Beautiful Bracelets By Hand

PAGE STREET
PUBLISHING CO.

First published in 2014 by
Page Street Publishing Co.
27 Congress Street, Suite 103
Salem, MA 01970
www.pagestreetpublishing.com

Distributed by Macmillan; sales in Canada by The Canadian Manda Group; distribution in Canada by The Jaguar Book Group.

17 16 15   2 3 4 5

ISBN-13: 978-1-62414-090-7
ISBN-10: 1-62414-090-4

Library of Congress Control Number: 2014939128

Cover and book design by Page Street Publishing Co.
Photography by Jade Gedeon

Printed and bound in U.S.A.

Page Street is proud to be a member of 1% for the Planet. Members donate one percent of their sales to one or more of the over 1,500 environmental and sustainability charities across the globe who participate in this program.

Beautiful Bracelets By Hand

SEVENTY–FIVE ONE–OF–A–KIND BAUBLES, BANGLES AND
OTHER WRIST ADORNMENTS YOU CAN MAKE AT HOME

JADE GEDEON

FOUNDER AND DESIGNER OF WE DREAM IN COLOUR WITH JEWELRY
FEATURED IN MORE THAN 800 BOUTIQUES AROUND THE WORLD

PAGE STREET
PUBLISHING CO.

CONTENTS

introduction

we dream in colour—like so many businesses—started quite by accident. constantly creating bits and baubles, my brooklyn flatmate and friend suggested we build a shared website as an outlet to sell our ever-growing collection. she left the site not long after to pursue a great career, but my line continued to grow and flourish thanks to the attention of great customers, wonderful blogs, amazing press and an incredible behind-the-scenes team. i don't pay much attention to marketing—i simply focus on making things that i love and hope others will enjoy. i still have friends elbow me when i'm complimented on my jewelry and i don't mention that i designed or sell it.

i'm thankful for such a brilliant opportunity to share the satisfaction of making beautiful things. jewelry has long been a means of personal expression, and thanks to ever-evolving materials and casual style challenging its traditional notions of stature, it continues to become more and more fun.

the projects in this book range in style, but they share a common link: the inimitable appeal of handicraft. one of the hallmarks of my line is the well-traveled look of the pieces. there is something undeniably appealing about the richness that things with age and patina bring to our lives, and whether by material or finish, many of the projects presented in this book reflect this notion. the materials used are affordable and easy to obtain, and there is endless room for personalization throughout the projects. i hope you have as much of a blast making each and every one of these as we did.

Beads

Long used for ornament and an early form of currency, beads have been traded globally for centuries and play an integral part in the development of commerce and economic networks. Our human ancestors began creating beads around 43,000 years ago, and you can seriously understand why small, beautiful objects just get your want genes tingling.

Gilded waves Bracelet

Be warned, the combination of cerulean tones and glimmering gold in this piece will have you daydreaming of sun-soaked sands and crystalline waters. Might as well give up on work and skip to the beach! When shopping for beads, line up your strands and play around until you get a pleasing variety of shapes and sizes.

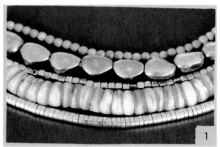

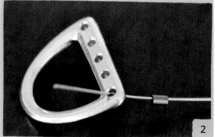

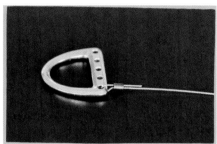

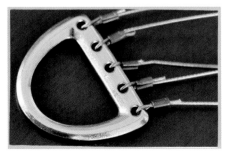

BITS YOU'LL NEED

- Ten gold-plated crimp bead covers
- Ten 3x2mm crimp tubes
- Three 7x5mm gold-plated jump rings, 18 gauge
- One five-strand gold-plated D-ring toggle clasp
- Five 9" (22.9 cm) strands of beading wire, 0.024" diameter
- Three strands of gold-plated beads (or raw brass) at least 7" (17.8 cm) long
- Two strands of turquoise glass beads at least 7" (17.8 cm) long

TOOLS

- Crimping pliers
- Wire snips
- Nylon-jaw pliers
- Chain-nose pliers
- Flat-nose pliers

1. Line up your strands in stringing order. Measure your wrist or a favorite bracelet, then subtract the length of the clasp, (don't forget the jump rings) to get the approximate length of your bead strands. Cut five pieces of beading wire that are 2 inches (5.1 cm) longer than your required length. This will give you extra room to work with.

2. Thread crimp onto wire, loop through clasp and thread back through crimp, leaving a short tail. Lay the tube in the first U-shaped notch of the crimping pliers. Taking care to keep the strands separated, squeeze closed to crimp. Move the crimped tube to the round opening. Turning 90 degrees, squeeze to secure. If tail is too long, trim carefully. Repeat for additional four strands.

3. String your largest strand first. Most beads need a little room to move, but if working with heishi (disc) beads, take care to allow extra space for the beads to flex when worn. Thread through the other end of the clasp with a crimp bead, but before crimping try it on to make sure it fits and moves correctly. Make any adjustments to length and extra room before crimping. String additional strands from next largest to smallest, checking each time for fit before crimping.

4. When all the strands are crimped on both ends, connect the toggle with jump rings, using pliers to close.

5. Slip crimp covers on one by one. Use a pair of nylon-jaw pliers to close them gently without marring the finish.

6. Plot which poolside/beach/island you'll wear this to first.

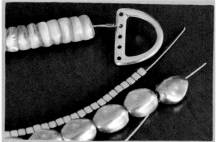

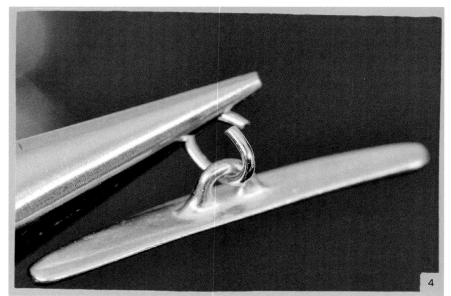

strata Bracelet

Finished with a tiny tassel, layers of luminescent hues will make you swoon every time you excavate this gemstone beauty from your jewel box. Ours is a mix of green onyx, smoky quartz, carnelian and labradorite.

BITS YOU'LL NEED

- 5½" (14 cm), or more, selection of coordinating 4x2mm faceted rondelle gemstone beads
- Two brass beads (hole must be larger than 2mm in diameter to fit over crimp tubes) or two crimp bead covers
- Two 3x2mm crimp tubes
- Four 5mm jump rings, 18–20 gauge
- One 4mm jump ring, 16–18 gauge
- One 4mm jump ring, 18–20 gauge
- One 9x5mm lobster clasp
- 9" (22.9 cm) length of beading wire, 0.014" diameter
- Spool of silk thread (you'll only need a small bit)
- Fray Check or clear nail polish

TOOLS

- Crimping pliers
- Wire snips
- Nylon-jaw pliers (if using crimp covers)
- Chain-nose pliers
- Flat-nose pliers
- Scissors
- Cardstock (an old business card works great!)

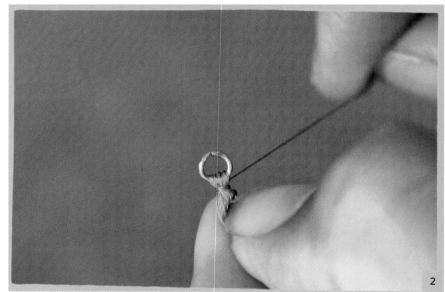

1. Make your itty-bitty tassel. Working with a ⅝-inch (1.6 cm) width of card, wrap your thread through a securely closed 4mm jump ring and around the card. Continue wrapping around fully about twenty times, then, grabbing firmly, slide off the card.

2. Wrap the string around the top of the tassel, just under the jump ring, about six times.

3. Loop thread through the last wrap and knot securely. Using a surgeon's knot (see techniques, page 211), knot again twice and dab knot with a bit of Fray Check or clear nail polish. Let dry and snip off excess string. Trim bottom of tassel.

4. Cut your beading wire 2 inches (5.1 cm) longer than your required length. This will give you extra room to work with. Thread and crimp your beading wire onto a securely closed 5mm jump ring. See techniques (page 209) for detailed instructions on crimping.

5. Thread your brass bead over the closed crimp tube to cover. If using crimp covers, slip them on and use a pair of nylon-jaw pliers to close them gently without marring the finish.

6. Thread the jump ring with tassel onto your wire.

7. Decide on your layout and string your beads. We strung our stones in (roughly) 1-inch (2.5 cm) lengths.

8. Unless using a crimp cover, thread brass bead and crimp tube onto free end of wire. Finish by looping wire through a securely closed 5mm jump ring, then crimp tube. This is a good time to test the length and adjust. Crimp to close and trim excess wire.

9. Attach two 5mm brass jump rings to one end, linking each to the other.

10. Attach the lobster clasp to the opposite end with a 4mm jump ring.

11. Congratulations. You are now a geogemjewelologist.

vertebrae bracelets

With endless options in color combinations, these work great as gifts for jewelry-wearing blokes. The African glass beads are shaped to mimic interlocking snake vertebrae and have a modern and edgy feel, despite their vintage origins.

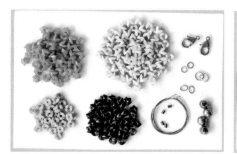

BITS YOU'LL NEED

- About 16" (40.6 cm) of assorted African glass snake trade beads (we used 9mm beads)
- Two 18x12mm lobster clasps
- Two 7x5mm brass jump rings, 16–18 gauge
- Two 9mm round jump rings, 16–18 gauge
- Two 5mm round jump rings, 16–18 gauge
- Two 9" (22.9 cm) lengths of beading wire, 0.024" diameter (longer for men or those with larger wrists)
- Four 3x2mm crimp tubes
- Four 9–12mm round brass beads (hole must be larger than 2 mm in diameter to fit over crimp tubes)

TOOLS

- Crimping pliers
- Wire snips
- Chain-nose pliers
- Flat-nose pliers

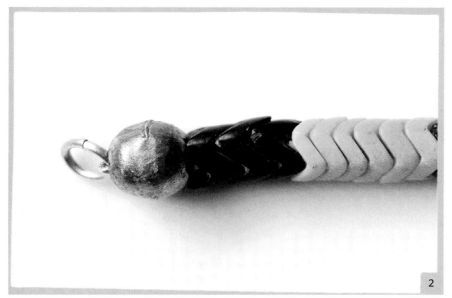

1. Once you've decided on your bead arrangement, cut two 9-inch (22.9 cm) lengths of beading wire. This will give you extra room to work with.

2. Thread and crimp your beading wire onto a securely closed 5mm jump ring. See techniques (page 209) for detailed instructions on crimping. Thread your first brass bead over the closed crimp tube and continue adding your glass beads.

3. When you've finished stringing your glass beads, add another brass bead to finish, then slip on your crimp tube and loop through a 7x5mm jump ring.

4. Bend your bracelet to determine how much slack you'll need to have the beads move comfortably. Once you're sure about how much extra room you need to leave (you're sure that you're sure, right?), crimp the tube closed.

5. Slide the brass bead over the crimp and snip off the extra tail.

6. Connect the jump ring to a lobster clasp.

7. Add the 9mm jump ring to the other end.

8. Repeat steps 1–7 for a second bracelet. Contemplate giving the second to a friend, but decide against it when you realize how great they look together.

coded Bracelet

Hide a message in your jewelry! We've used three beads to represent a dash, but you can substitute tube beads if you please. You can also choose beads with a more daring contrast to make your message pop. Depending on the size of your beads (and wrist), you should be able to fit three to six characters—your choice of word (or acronym) will be dictated slightly by your wrist and bead size.

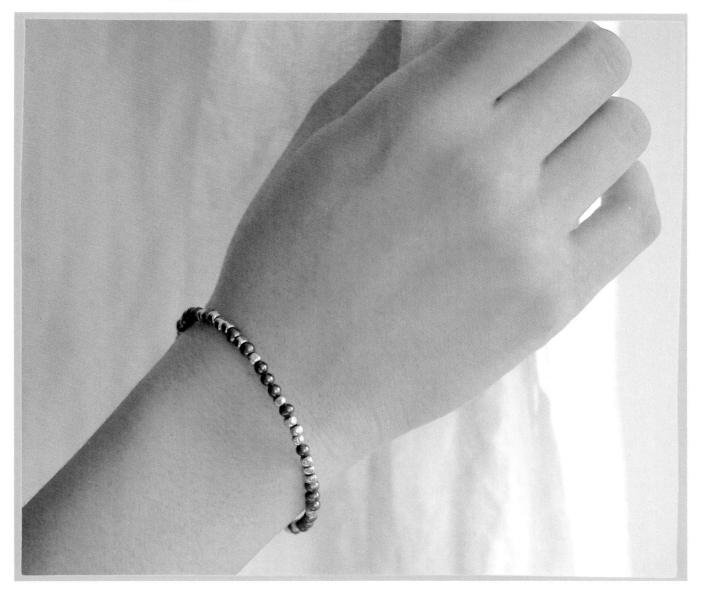

BITS YOU'LL NEED

- Beads (we used 4mm round brass and pearls)
- Two crimp bead covers
- Two 3x2mm crimp tubes
- One 12x8mm lobster clasp
- One 7mm brass jump ring, 16–18 gauge
- One 6x4mm brass jump ring, 16–18 gauge
- 9" (22.9 cm) length of beading wire, 0.014" diameter

TOOLS

- Crimping pliers
- Wire snips
- Nylon-jaw pliers (if using crimp covers)
- Chain-nose pliers
- Flat-nose pliers

1. Subtracting 1 inch (2.5 cm) for findings, measure your wrist or a favorite bracelet to get your beading length. Calculate how many beads will fit on this length and play with the characters to determine what you'd like to say and if it can fit. We fit five characters on ours. Pearls represent the dots and dashes while the brass acts as the pause. One pearl is a dot, and three a dash. One brass bead is a quick pause within a character, and three a space between characters.

2. Cut your beading wire 2 inches (5.1 cm) longer than your required length. This will give you extra room to work with. Attach the lobster clasp to a 6x4mm jump ring and close securely, then thread and crimp your beading wire onto the jump ring. See techniques (page 209) for detailed instructions on crimping.

3. String your beads.

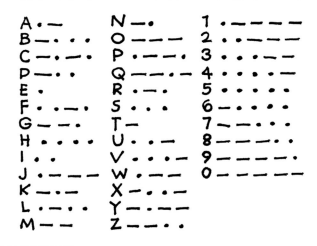

INTERNATIONAL MORSE CODE

A ·—	N —·	1 ·————
B —···	O ———	2 ··———
C —·—·	P ·——·	3 ···——
D —··	Q ——·—	4 ····—
E ·	R ·—·	5 ·····
F ··—·	S ···	6 —····
G ——·	T —	7 ——···
H ····	U ··—	8 ———··
I ··	V ···—	9 ————·
J ·———	W ·——	0 —————
K —·—	X —··—	
L ·—··	Y —·——	
M ——	Z ——··	

1

3

4. Thread brass bead and crimp tube onto free end of wire. Finish by looping wire through the 7mm jump ring, then crimp tube. This is a good time to test the length and adjust. Most beads need a little room to move when the bracelet is flexed. Crimp to close and trim excess wire.

5. Slip crimp covers on one by one. Use a pair of nylon-jaw pliers to close them gently without marring the finish.

6. Show off to a friend. If they can decipher your message with a single glance, then you might be friends with Jason Bourne.

raku Handpiece

There is something gorgeous about the rustic earthy finish of raku ceramics. The handmade scarab bead we used was purchased from Wondrous Strange on Etsy and has a beautiful iridescent sheen. You can substitute another focal shape or material, but it will need to have three attachment points. Many of the makers will happily add loops to a different bead or customize an alternate design for you, so have a bit of fun with it.

BITS YOU'LL NEED

- Focal bead (ours is 2" x ¾" [5.1 x 1.9 cm])
- 12" (30.5 cm) length of chain (we used 9" [22.9 cm], but you might need a bit more depending on the size of your focal and hand)
- Ten 6mm jump rings, 16–18 gauge
- One 12x8mm lobster clasp

TOOLS

- Metal shears or wire snips
- Chain-nose pliers
- Flat-nose pliers

1. Measure carefully, then cut your chain lengths. Cut your lengths a bit longer than you think you need—you can always trim them back. For our piece we used two 2-inch (5.1 cm) pieces to go around the wrist, one 2-inch (5.1 cm) piece for the ring and one 3-inch (7.6 cm) piece to connect the ring to the base of the focal. Drape the chain around your finger to determine the length, making sure it can move easily over your knuckles.

2. Lay out your piece.

3. Assemble the ring chain first by looping onto a jump ring. Make sure there are no kinks or twists. Add the connector chain before closing.

4. Attach the connector chain to the base of your focal and the other two lengths to the sides. Finish with a jump ring extender on one end, linking one to the chain and each successive jump ring to the next. Attach the lobster clasp to the other end with a jump ring. Try it on and tweak if necessary.

ombre Bracelet

A dip-dyed effect elevates this simple strand from subtle to sublime. For ease we've used a presorted length of graduated-color smoky quartz. When shopping, search for shaded gemstone strands. You can also create your own ombre effect with different shades of glass or crystal beads.

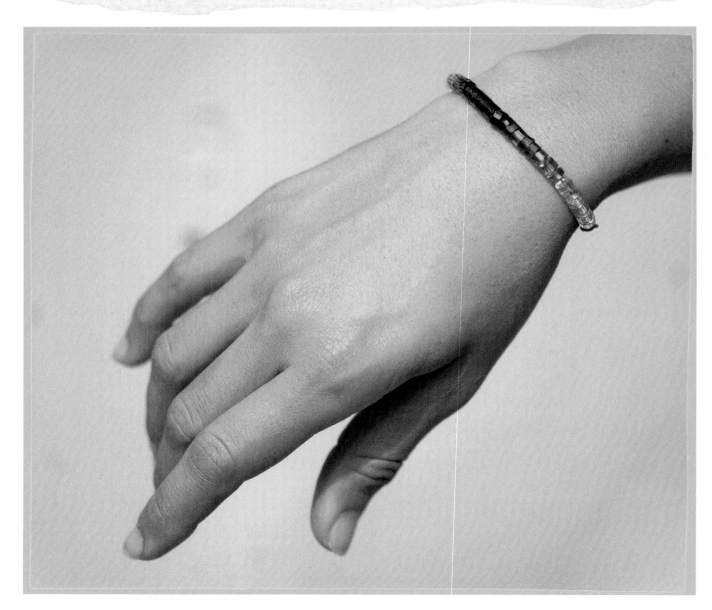

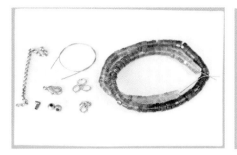

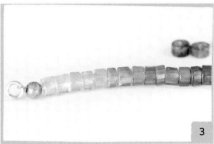

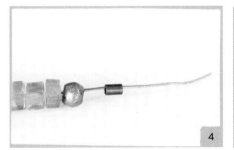
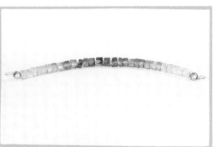

BITS YOU'LL NEED

- 3¾" (9.5 cm) length of shaded beads (we used 5x3mm heishi)
- 2" (5.1 cm) length of chain
- Two 4mm round brass beads (hole must be larger than 2 mm in diameter to fit over crimp tubes) or crimp bead covers
- Two 3x2mm crimp tubes
- One 12x8mm lobster clasp
- Three 4mm brass jump rings, 16–18 gauge
- Three 6x4mm brass jump rings, 16–18 gauge
- 6" (15.2 cm) length of beading wire, 0.014" diameter

TOOLS

- Crimping pliers
- Wire snips
- Nylon-jaw pliers (if using crimp covers)
- Chain-nose pliers
- Flat-nose pliers

1. Thread and crimp your beading wire onto a securely closed 4mm jump ring. See techniques (page 209) for detailed instructions on crimping. Thread your first brass bead over the closed crimp tube. If using crimp covers, slip them on and use a pair of nylon-jaw pliers to close them gently without marring the finish.

2. Arrange your selected beads.

3. Thread your beads on in order.

4. Thread brass bead (unless you are using crimp covers) and crimp tube onto wire. Finish by looping wire through a 4mm jump ring, then crimp tube. This is a good time to test the length and adjust. Most beads need a little room to move, but if working with heishi (disc) beads, take care to allow extra space for the beads to flex when worn. Crimp to close and trim excess wire.

5. Attach chain to one end with a 6x4mm jump ring.

6. Attach clasp to the other end of the chain with a 4mm jump ring.

7. Attach two 6x4mm jump rings to the other end of your bead strand.

8. Done!

Beribboned Bracelet

A perfectly simple formula that easily fits many wrists. We used opalescent glass and cool teal ribbon, but you can play with color, texture, shape and size for infinite variations.

BITS YOU'LL NEED

- 5' (152.4 cm) length of of ¼" (6 mm) ribbon (or 2½' [76.2 cm] if using a single strand of a thicker ribbon)
- 6" (15.2 cm) length of 12mm round beads
- Two to four brass beads (hole must be larger than 2mm in diameter to fit over crimp tubes) or two crimp bead covers
- Two 3x2mm crimp tubes
- Four 5.5mm brass jump rings, 20 gauge
- Two 7mm brass jump rings, 18 gauge (larger for thicker ribbons)
- 9" (22.9 cm) length of beading wire, 0.024" diameter
- Fray Check or clear nail polish

TOOLS

- Crimping pliers
- Wire snips
- Nylon-jaw pliers (if using crimp covers)
- Chain-nose pliers
- Flat-nose pliers
- Scissors

1. Cut four 14-inch (35.6 cm) lengths of ribbon. Dab the edges with Fray Check or clear nail polish to seal so they won't unravel. Let dry.

2. Cut your beading wire 2 inches (5.1 cm) longer than your required length. This will give you extra room to work with. Thread and crimp your beading wire onto two securely closed 5.5mm jump rings. See techniques (page 209) for detailed instructions on crimping.

3. Thread your brass bead (or beads) over the closed crimp tube to cover. If using crimp covers, slip them on and use a pair of nylon-jaw pliers to close them gently without marring the finish.

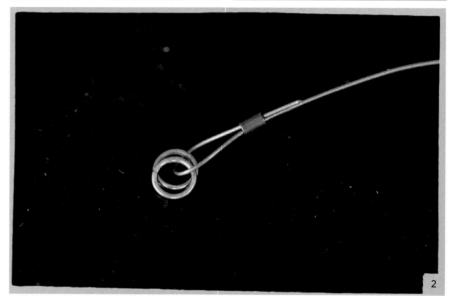

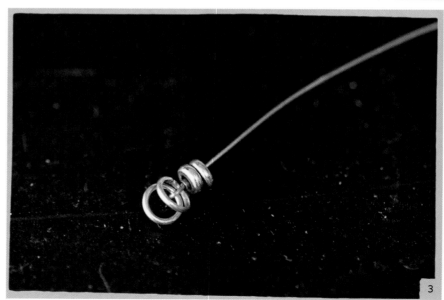

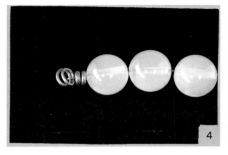

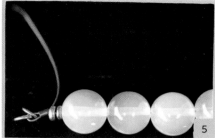

4. String your beads.

5. Thread brass bead (unless using crimp cover) and crimp tube onto free end of wire. Finish by looping wire through two securely closed 5.5mm jump rings, then crimp tube. This is a good time to test the length and adjust. Most beads need a little room to move when the bracelet is flexed. Crimp to close and trim excess wire.

6. Attach the 7mm brass jump rings to each end, through both smaller jump rings.

7. Thread your ribbon through the 7mm jump ring.

8. Using both ribbons, form an overhand knot close to the jump rings. Do this on each side. See techniques (page 211).

9. Tie a bow to close, preferably on your wrist.

vinyl Heishi Bracelet

These sequin-style African heishi beads were originally made from vulcanite, but you can easily and affordably find vinyl versions in a great assortment of vibrant colors. Create stacks of different solids or mix hues up within each bracelet for an entirely different feel.

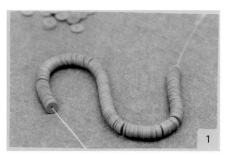

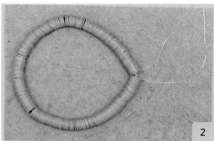

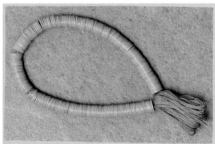

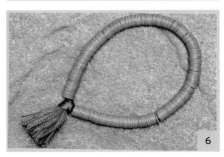

BITS YOU'LL NEED

- 8" (20.3 cm) strand of vinyl heishi beads per bracelet (we used 6mm beads)
- One skein of embroidery floss
- 12" (30.5 cm) length of elastic cord
- E6000 adhesive
- Cardstock (an old business card works well)

TOOLS

- Scissors

1. Give the elastic cord a good stretch (see techniques, page 209) and knot one end to keep beads from slipping off as you string them. To speed things up, you can grab beads off the original strand in a chunk between your index finger and thumb, and slip the cord through that, rather than threading the beads one by one.

2. When fully strung to desired length, knot, knot and knot again. See stretching cord (page 209) for detailed instructions.

3. Fold or cut a piece of cardstock to desired length of tassel (ours is about 1 inch [2.5 cm]). Wrap floss over knot and card until you've got a good thickness. We wrapped ours about twenty-two times around.

4. Holding floss together securely, bend the card and slip it out.

5. Use an 8-inch (20.3 cm) length of floss and a whipping knot to secure. See techniques (page 211) for detailed instructions.

6. Trim end of tassel.

Bits + Pieces

A little bit of everything, these projects feature an inspiring mix of materials. Most you can quickly find in shops or online. The antique, vintage and one-of-a-kind finds used, culled for their inimitable charm and darned good looks, might take a bit more perusing on your part, but I'm not lying when I say that shopping for beautiful old goodies is a massive part of the fun—especially when it gets you on your feet and wandering the markets. You might even have a few of these items gathering dust in your collections, waiting for a new incarnation.

buckle Bracelet

Opulent old shoe and sash buckles make a historical statement in this new incarnation. When shopping for buckles, keep an eye out for bold sizes and a base structure that you can easily link jump rings and chain to. While we list approximate sizes and lengths, your buckle size will dictate how much chain you need.

BITS YOU'LL NEED

- One buckle
- 5"–10" (12.7–25.4 cm) length of chunky unsoldered chain (you should see a seam on each link)
- 1"–2" (2.5–5.1 cm) length of slightly chunkier unsoldered chain or jump rings for extender
- One lobster clasp (ours is 20mm long)

TOOLS

- File
- Sprue cutters or heavy-duty wire cutters
- Chain-nose pliers
- Flat-nose pliers

1. Prep your focal piece. If your buckle has a center bar and pin, you'll need to remove them and file down the connection so it lies comfortably against your wrist. Use a sprue (or heavy-duty wire) cutter to nip off the bar as close as you can get to the connection (you can also use a jeweler's saw) and file the remaining metal until smooth. If necessary, bend the frame gently to fit the curve of your wrist.

2. Here's the vaguely tricky bit. Since every buckle will have slightly different dimensions, you'll have to lay out your buckle, determine the total desired length of your bracelet and calculate the necessary lengths of chain to meet your desired overall measurements. Our bracelet has two lengths of chain on each side that meet to form a triangle as well as a small tail of chunkier chain that will act as our extender and clasp connection.

3. Using pliers, gently open the chain links and separate your required lengths.

4. Close the chain links, connecting the chains to your buckle.

5. Connect the extender of the chunkier chain to one end of your bracelet, linking your two chain ends to form a triangle. Take care to keep the links neat and parallel so they lie attractively and don't twist when worn. Attach the lobster clasp to the other end. Adjust length if necessary.

6. Revel in your one-of-a-kind awesomeness.

great glitter bracelet

Party perfect and infinitely glam, these bold sparkling links make quite an impact. We dissected some unsoldered chain and used it to link our pieces along with jump rings, but you can also just use jump rings if you like. Don't be shy—get fancy and alter the chain and findings to match the links you select.

BITS YOU'LL NEED

- Rhinestone links with four rear connections (we used four pieces with 1" [2.5 cm] diameter)
- Four lengths of 2x4mm chain (we used 1" [2.5 cm] pieces)
- 1"–2" (2.5–5.1 cm) length of 5x7mm unsoldered chain (to take apart and use as links)
- Twenty-four 4mm jump rings, 16 gauge (if you are not using chain to connect links; otherwise, use eighteen)
- Toggle clasp

TOOLS

- Chain-nose pliers
- Flat-nose pliers

1. Using pliers, separate 5x7mm chain links (or use jump rings). Connect two 4mm jump rings to the chain link and then connect the 4mm jump rings to the rhinestone links. Be sure to keep your links parallel. Repeat again for the second connection.

2. Repeat this process, connecting each rhinestone link until complete.

3. Check your measurements to determine how much chain you'll need to connect to the clasp. The chain will form a triangle once the clasp is attached.

4. Using 4mm jump rings, connect the chains to the end rhinestone links and then attach the toggle to the two free chain ends.

5. Repeat on the other side to finish and attach the toggle bar.

6. Go forth and sparkle plenty!

brooch bracelet

I often stumble across beautiful old brooches that aren't suitable for drilling, and this is a swift and easy way to give them new purpose. Styles with a simple C catch and pin work best as you can easily secure the pin without damaging the face of the brooch. If you can find vintage chain or components that match the look of your piece, better yet. Keep an eye out for damaged vintage jewelry you can play chop shop with.

BITS YOU'LL NEED

- One brooch (with C catch)
- Chain
- One 10x6mm lobster clasp
- Five 5mm round jump rings, 16–18 gauge
- One 4mm round jump ring, 16–18 gauge
- Painter's tape

TOOLS

- Wire snips
- Chain-nose pliers
- Flat-nose pliers

1. Wrap half of your plier nose with a few rounds of painter's tape. This will help protect the front face of your brooch. With the bare side on the rear and masked on the front, gently squeeze the catch down to tighten.

2. Remove the tape and use the pliers to squeeze the catch from the side until pin is secure and immobilized. Measure the length of your bar and subtract it from your total desired length of your bracelet. Halve that and cut two pieces of chain to that length. Don't fret too much—you can always add a jump ring or two to extend or trim the chain to fit.

3. Attach each length of chain to the pin with a 5mm jump ring.

4. Attach the lobster clasp with the 4mm jump ring to one end. Finish the other end of the bracelet with the remaining three jump rings, linking each to the other.

5. Try on and then try to exercise restraint every time you spy a cute old pin—or sixty-two—at an antiques fair. You don't have to buy them all. I haven't succeeded with the restraint bit, but perhaps you will.

rhinestone Fringe Bangle

We used vintage rectangular rhinestone drops that we procured on Etsy, but you can easily find newer versions in craft shops and online, so search for something you love. This ranks a step higher on the difficulty scale than the Tremblant Bangle (page 48) since you'll have to get handy with a drill.

BITS YOU'LL NEED

- One thin brass bangle (ours is ⅛" [3 mm] high and ¹⁄₁₆" [1.6 mm] thick—a little thinner would be lovely, but thicker becomes more difficult to drill!)
- Enough rhinestone drops to span a 2½" (6.4 cm) width when lined up side by side (ours are 7x12mm)
- 4.5mm jump rings, 18 gauge (enough to connect your rhinestone drops)
- 100-grit sandpaper

TOOLS

- Jeweler's automatic center punch
- Drill
- Safety glasses
- Hammer
- #54 or #55 drill bit
- Chain-nose pliers
- Flat-nose pliers

1. Line your drops up against the bangle, shoulder to shoulder, and mark the drill points.

2. Flipping the bangle to its broad side, and aligning with the marks on the top, use a center punch and a little hammer tap to indent the metal in the center of the band where you'd like to drill. Get your supercool safety glasses on and drill away. The center punch mark will give your bit a nice starting point so it doesn't travel all over the surface of your bangle. You can sand the bracelet to even out the surface if necessary.

3. With both pairs of pliers, twist open a jump ring and slip a drop on. Make sure it is facing the proper direction. Close the jump ring and continue attaching the rest of your drops.

4. Admire.

POINTS of Light Bracelet

Petite glimmering glass links illuminate simple chain for a sweet and subtle piece perfect for layering. You'll need connector bits with two loops—one on either end—and bar chain you can disassemble.

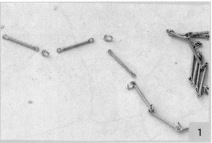

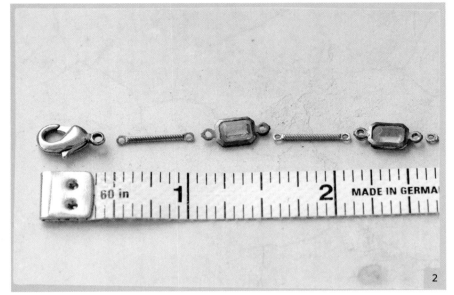

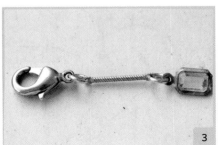

BITS YOU'LL NEED

- Tiny glass or rhinestone connectors (we used five, each 10mm wide)
- 5"–7" (12.7–17.8 cm) of bar chain (our bars were 10mm long)
- Twelve (or more) 3mm round jump rings, 18–20 gauge
- One 5mm round jump ring, 16–18 gauge
- One 9x6mm lobster clasp

TOOLS

- Metal shears or wire snips
- Chain-nose pliers
- Flat-nose pliers

1. You'll be using the bar portion of your chain, so you can cut or open and remove the small jump rings connecting them until you have a few links ready to go.

2. A ruler or tape measure is handy to help you approximate how many links and connectors you'll need. Lay out your pieces and continue to separate chain links until you've reached your desired length.

3. Attach your lobster clasp with a 3mm jump ring to your first link, and continue to link your pieces together with 3mm jump rings—building your chain—until you've reached the end.

4. Attach the 5mm jump ring to the end to complete.

5. Pretty, huh?

crystal clear bracelet

Chandelier crystals do a beautiful job of refracting light—as they're meant to, of course. This bracelet will infuse your look with a spark of razzle-dazzle and a cool vintage vibe. Look for crystals that still have their head pins intact. Choose a clasp size that best coordinates with the scale of your crystals. You will need more jump rings if using smaller crystals.

BITS YOU'LL NEED

- 5"–6" (12.7–15.2 cm) length of chandelier crystals (ours are 1" [2.5 cm] across)
- Three 10mm round jump rings, 16–18 gauge
- Seven 6mm round jump rings, 16–18 gauge
- One lobster clasp (ours is 25mm long)
- Head pins (optional)

TOOLS

- Wire snips
- Chain-nose pliers
- Flat-nose pliers
- Round-nose pliers

1. Using the round-nose pliers, grasp the end of a head pin wire and roll it around the plier nose to form a closed loop. If the pins are excessively long, you may need to trim them.

2. Begin linking your crystals with the 6mm jump rings. Be sure to keep everything parallel.

3. When all the crystals are linked, attach the clasp to one end with two 6mm jump rings.

4. Attach the three 10mm jump rings to each other and then attach to the other end of the bracelet with a 6mm jump ring.

5. This is what it should look like on the back.

6. Shine on!

itty-Bitty Halo Bracelet

Suspended on superfine chain, a darling circle of glinting gems takes center stage.

BITS YOU'LL NEED

- One 12mm rhinestone ring
- 15"–17" (38.1–43.2 cm) length of 1–1.5mm chain
- One 7x5mm brass jump ring, 16–18 gauge
- Two 4mm jump rings, 18–22 gauge
- One 9x6mm lobster clasp

TOOLS

- Metal shears or wire snips
- Chain-nose pliers
- Flat-nose pliers

1. Decide on the length of your bracelet and measure how much chain you'll need for each side. Since you'll be making a lark's head knot (see techniques, page 211) with the chain to link it to the ring, you'll need to double up your chain and add a little extra length to compensate.

2. Cut two lengths of chain to size. They should each be around 7 inches (17.8 cm) long (you can always trim the excess to fit).

3. Make a lark's head knot and join the loose ends of chain with a 4mm jump ring.

4. Repeat with the second chain, adding your lobster clasp to one end and the 7x5mm jump ring to the other.

5. Feel perfectly angelic.

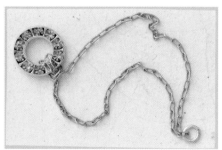

tremblant Bangle

Tiny gems tremble and dance as you move, giving you ample opportunities to sparkle. Feel free to substitute alternate colored drops in this swift and easy assembly if pink isn't your thing.

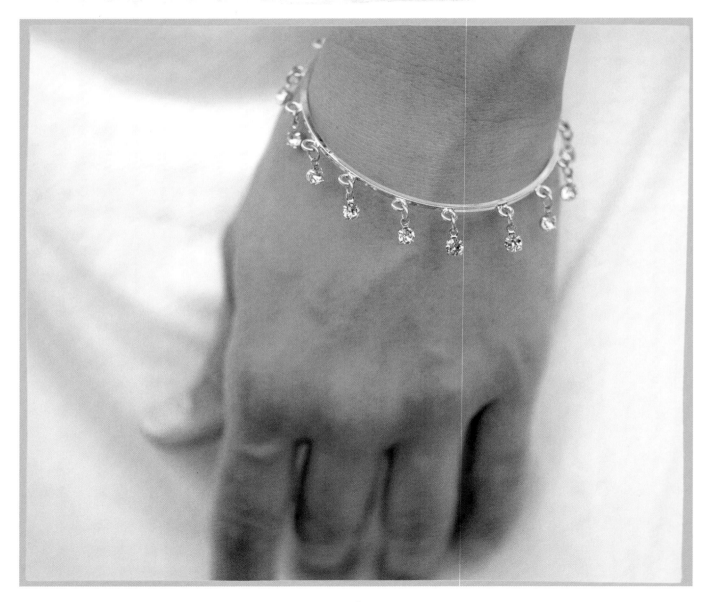

BITS YOU'LL NEED

- Sixteen Swarovski 4–4.1mm round drops
- One bangle with sixteen loops (sizes vary, so pick what is best for you!)
- Sixteen 4mm jump rings, 16–18 gauge (extra jump rings are always good!)

TOOLS

- Chain-nose pliers
- Flat-nose pliers

1. With both pairs of pliers, twist open a jump ring and slip a drop on. Make sure it is facing the proper direction.

2. Close the jump ring and continue attaching the rest of your drops until you've come full circle.

3. Shimmy, shake, sparkle.

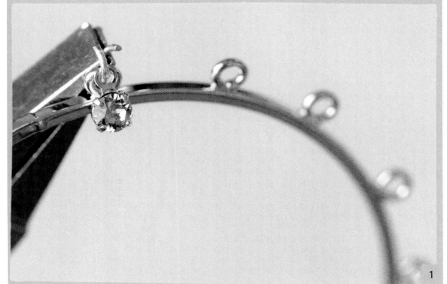

assemblage bracelet

Take a vintage (or new, no judgment here) sparkler, add a dash of ribbon, a splash of ornament and mix together for a one-of-a-kind wonder that's all your own. Wider bracelets with rows of rhinestones or rhinestone and chain links work best as a base (versus a single strand) onto which to weave your fixin's.

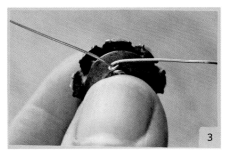

BITS YOU'LL NEED

- Rhinestone bracelet
- Ribbon (choose a width that is visually balanced with your bracelet—we used ¾" [1.9 cm] ribbon for a bracelet that was just under ½" [1.3 cm] wide)
- Selection of buttons, small pins, rhinestone connectors or charms
- Wire, 24–26 gauge
- Fray Check

TOOLS

- Chain-nose pliers
- Flat-nose pliers
- Wire snips
- Scissors

1. Lay out your components and play with your design until you are content.

2. Tie a classic bow with your ribbon (see techniques, page 211). Before pulling completely tight, insert a 4-inch (10.2 cm) length of wire through the back. Finish ends with a bit of Fray Check to keep from unraveling.

3. Begin stitching on your elements with wire, beginning with a few wraps at your starting point.

4. Attaching the largest component first, continue working to fill in around it with smaller components. Use pliers to pull your wire through and keep taut as you work. After the last component is secured, loop wire around your bracelet a few times once again and trim.

5. When all your components are attached, wire your ribbon on.

6. Receive diploma in jewelry doctoring.

chandelier drop bracelet

A few stylish steps away from their already glamorous roots, chunky chandelier crystals gleam in this fun statement-maker piece. We've used a vintage blue baroque-cut crystal, but Swarovski makes a wealth of colors and sizes you can play with.

BITS YOU'LL NEED

• Nine to twelve 1½" (3.8 cm)-long chandelier prisms

• 7" (17.8 cm) length of chunky chain (we used 9mm chain)

• Ten to twelve 10mm jump rings, 18–20 gauge (check the size of your prism hole)

• Three 22mm jump rings, 14–16 gauge

• One 7mm jump ring, 16–18 gauge

• One 18x10mm lobster clasp

TOOLS

• Chain-nose pliers
• Flat-nose pliers

1. Thread your jump ring through the hole in the crystal. Make sure it moves easily. If you need to use a smaller gauge ring, please do; otherwise, forcing it may cause the crystals to break or chip.

2. Add your first crystal to the center of your chain.

3. Determine how far you'd like to space the pieces and continue adding them, taking care to keep your links and jump rings parallel for each new addition.

4. Add the clasp to one end with a 7mm jump ring.

5. Attach the three 22mm jump rings one by one to the other end of your chain, linking each to the other.

6. Shake it, don't break it—but do tell everyone that you made it.

button Bracelet

Anyone else out there guilty of collecting buttons? Anyone? Anyone? Now is the time to admit it. Of the myriad bits and bobs floating around my vintage and antique collection, buttons are repping hard. This is a great way to show them some love. You'll want to use buttons with a raised shank on the rear.

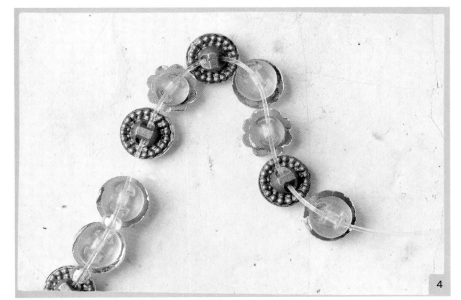

BITS YOU'LL NEED

- 1mm clear beading elastic
- Buttons (we used twenty-six ¾" [1.8 cm] and three 10–12mm buttons)
- Coordinating spacer beads (we used eighteen 4mm glass seed beads)
- E6000 adhesive

TOOLS

- Scissors

1. Cut a length of elastic 4 inches (10.2 cm) longer than your desired length. Give it a good stretch (see techniques, page 209) and knot one end to keep the beads and buttons from slipping off as you string them.

2. Play with your arrangement.

3. Start stringing. For the front of the bracelet, we added spacer beads between the buttons so more of their faces are visible when worn.

4. Toward the ends we omitted spacer beads, which will allow the buttons to rotate and cluster.

5. When fully strung, knot, knot and knot again. See techniques (page 211) for detailed instructions.

6. Slip it on.

montee Bracelet

Delicate chain is punctuated by lustrous sewing findings. Montee is a type of rhinestone setting that allows you to sew through the back to stitch it onto fabric. Vintage montees are especially beautiful, as they often have a great patina to the setting and aged mottle to the foil that gives the piece an heirloom feel.

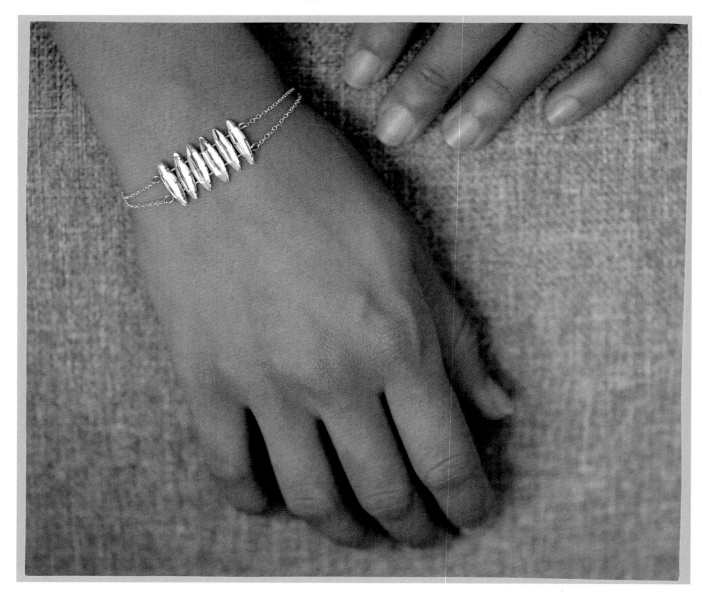

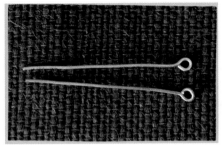

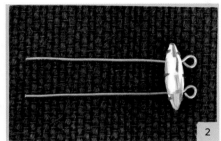

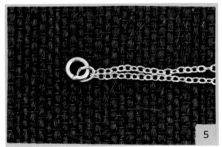

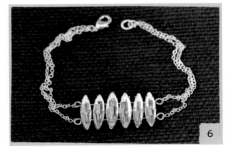

BITS YOU'LL NEED

- Six 17x5mm double channel navette montees
- 14" (35.6 cm) length of 2mm chain
- Two 40mm lengths of wire, 16–18 gauge
- One 6mm jump ring, 16–18 gauge
- Two 4x3mm jump rings, 18–22 gauge
- One 9x6mm lobster clasp

TOOLS

- Metal shears or wire snips
- Round-nose pliers
- Chain-nose pliers
- Flat-nose pliers

1. Curl one end of each wire to form a small loop.

2. Thread your montees onto both wires.

3. Curl the ends to form a small loop and secure your montees.

4. Measure your piece and determine how much chain you'll need on each side. We used 2¾-inch (7 cm) pieces, but you may need to go a bit longer or shorter to fit. Cut four lengths and attach each by opening a loop, slipping on and closing again.

5. Line your chains up on each end and attach with a 4x3mm jump ring. Attach the clasp to one end and the 6mm jump ring to the other.

6. All done!

Hat Pin Bangle

Every time I visit an antiques market I come across a few particularly pretty hat pins. Instead of letting them collect dust, you can quickly fashion them into delicate bangles and wear your collection as it grows. You can find a wealth of them online as well. Pins with a flat head or smaller focal wear best.

BITS YOU'LL NEED

• One hat pin (pin stem should be 8" [20.3 cm] or longer)

TOOLS

• File
• Round-nose pliers
• Chain-nose pliers
• Flat-nose pliers
• Heavy-duty wire cutters

1. With a pair of chain-nose pliers, grasp the pin stem just below the joint. Using the flat-nose pliers, bend the pin to a 90-degree angle. Working from your bend to the end, gently and evenly bend the wire into a curve with your fingers.

2. Try it on. When you squeeze the end to make contact with the joint at the base of the pin it should fit comfortably, but overlap by ½ inch (1.3 cm). You'll be bending this bit to make a catch. If your pin is too long, you'll want to trim it. We'll skip ahead to show what you are aiming for.

3. File the end of your pin so it is no longer sharp (or rough if you've trimmed it).

4. Using the round-nose pliers, curve the end of the pin over, leaving a small gap so that you can easily hook it onto the wire at the base of the focal.

5. Here's what it should look like open.

6. And closed.

Little mysteries bracelet

One, two, three, four and even more ladylike lockets are lovingly linked for an enduringly beautiful statement. Keep special memories close or create a bespoke keepsake for a friend by tucking sweet somethings into each and every locket.

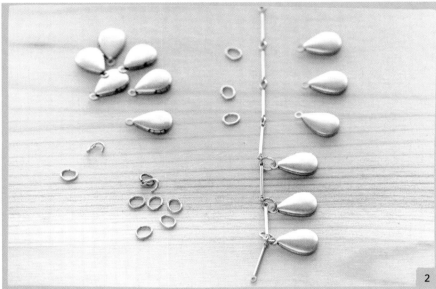

BITS YOU'LL NEED

- Tiny brass lockets (we used twelve, each ½" [1.3 cm] tall)
- 7" (17.8 cm) length of brass bar chain
- Three or four 7mm round brass jump rings, 18–20 gauge
- Twelve 5x4mm jump rings, 18–20 gauge (extra jump rings are always good!)
- One 5mm round jump ring, 18–20 gauge
- One lobster clasp (12mm)

TOOLS

- Chain-nose pliers
- Flat-nose pliers

1. Depending on your chain and desired spacing and length, you may need more (or fewer) lockets. If you plan on using larger lockets, choose an equally substantial chain, jump rings and clasp to balance the piece visually.

2. With 5x4mm jump rings, attach your lockets one by one to the chain at your desired intervals, taking care to keep the locket fronts all facing in the same direction. Be sure to link to the same side of the chain ring so they hang evenly.

3. All lockets attached? Yes? Great.

4. Attach the lobster clasp with a 5mm jump ring to one end.

5. Link the three 7mm jump rings to the other end to form your extender.

6. For bonus points, fill lockets with lovely little things.

teeny–weeny charm bracelet

This dainty bracelet is perfect for keeping things stylishly light. Keep it inexpensive and fun or dress it up with precious stones and metals.

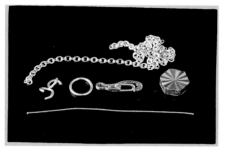

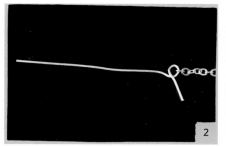

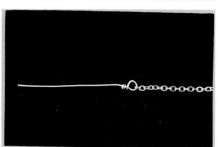

BITS YOU'LL NEED

• One very small charm (with a hole through the center) or bead (4–6mm is optimal)
• 7"–8" (17.8–20.3 cm) length of 1–1.5mm chain
• 2" (5.1 cm) length of 22-gauge wire
• One 7mm jump ring, 16–18 gauge
• Two 4mm jump rings, 18–22 gauge
• One 8x3mm self-closing clasp

TOOLS

• Metal shears or wire snips
• Round-nose pliers
• Chain-nose pliers
• Flat-nose pliers

1. Cut two lengths of chain, approximately 3½ inches (8.9 cm) long each. You may need more or less depending on your wrist.

2. Thread one end of your wire through the end of a length of chain and make a wrapped loop to link (see techniques, page 210).

3. Thread your bead or charm onto the wire and thread the wire through the end of your other length of chain and form another wrapped loop.

4. Add the clasp to one end with a 4mm jump ring and then use the second 4mm ring to attach the 7mm jump ring to the opposite end.

5. Teeny-weeny wonderful!

bright blossom bracelet

Available in a bevy of beautiful colors, plastic flower cabochons are easily drilled and turned into links. We set our flowers with point-back rhinestones, but you can skip the extra step and glue on flat backs if you choose. You can also add leaves or extra flower charms as drops from the connecting links. Adjust quantities, rhinestone size and findings for your particular size and shape of flower.

BITS YOU'LL NEED

- Six 20mm plastic (or resin) cabochons
- Six 3mm rhinestones
- Twelve 6mm jump rings, 18–20 gauge
- Five 5mm jump rings, 16–18 gauge
- Two 5x3mm jump rings, 16–18 gauge
- One 7.5mm button clasp
- Pasco Fix or similar instant-drying adhesive

TOOLS

- Chain-nose pliers
- Flat-nose pliers
- Drill
- #52 drill bit
- Safety glasses

1. Taking care not to drill too close to the edge, drill holes on opposite sides of your cabochon. If you are using point-back rhinestones, drill a small indentation where you'd like your stone placed. Take care to only drill a little way down, just past the point of the drill bit. Try fitting your stone and etch out a bit more space if necessary. If using flat-back stones, skip this step.

2. Glue your stone in (or on, for flat backs).

3. Repeat steps 1 and 2 until all stones are set.

4. Attach 6mm jump rings to both ends of your flowers.

5. When all the flowers have jump rings attached, link them together with 5mm jump rings, keeping everything parallel.

6. Attach each part of your button clasp to either end with a 5x3mm jump ring.

7. Finally, flowers that won't wilt in a week.

fresh-picked bracelet

Just the right amount of kitsch and ridiculously fun, this is a great use for all the vintage millinery fruit floating around. Search online and you will find a bounty of varieties to play with, but pay attention to the size before ordering so you don't end up with life-size fruit. The pieces used in this bracelet are just under 1 inch (2.5 cm) long. Also look for individually wired stems— they're often sold loose or wrapped in little clusters you can easily untwist.

BITS YOU'LL NEED

• Millinery fruit stems (we used thirteen, but you may need more or fewer depending on size and shape)
• 7" (17.8 cm) length of chain (something with a basket weave look is perfect)
• One 12mm toggle clasp
• Three 8x6mm jump rings, 16–18 gauge

TOOLS

• Wire snips
• Chain-nose pliers
• Flat-nose pliers

1. Straighten out your stems, then decide how many pieces you'd like to use and how you'd like them spaced along your length of chain.

2. Once you've figured out your spacing, thread the first wire through your chain.

3. Bend the wire over and down toward the fruit. The wire should be about ½ inch (1.3 cm) long from the top of the bend to the top of the fruit.

4. Bring the bent wire around the back of the other wire and begin wrapping to form a loop at the top.

5. If your wire is excessively long, trim it to about 1½ inches (3.8 cm) to make it easier to work with.

6. Using the chain-nose pliers, grasp the end of the wire and continue wrapping tightly around until you've hit the top of the fruit or have run out of wire to wrap. Trim if necessary.

7. Once you've finished, continue adding fruit until the entire length of chain is loaded.

8. Attach one jump ring to the toggle and close, and then attach with a second jump ring to the bracelet end.

9. Attach the hoop to the other end with the last jump ring.

10. Delicious!

collage bracelet

An assemblage of vintage metal and plastic flowers, an old tin pin (search for Japan/Japanese tin pins on Etsy and eBay) and rhinestones set on saturated ribbon make a playful, vibrant accessory. We found our flowers at Isabella's Collections on Etsy.

BITS YOU'LL NEED

- One vintage tin insect pin
- One to three metal flowers (depending on size—ours are 1¼" [32 mm] in diameter)
- One to three beads (to sit in the middle of your flowers, make sure the holes are large enough to sew through)
- Three flat-back rhinestones and tiffany rhinestone settings (since we used vintage rhinestones that were not flat back, we inverted ring settings to accommodate them)
- 6" (15.2 cm) length of 1½" (3.8 cm)-wide ribbon
- Two 19x5mm ribbon crimp ends
- One 6mm jump ring, 16–18 gauge
- Three 9x6mm jump rings, 16–18 gauge
- One 12x6mm lobster clasp
- Thread

TOOLS

- Scissors
- Chain-nose pliers
- Flat-nose pliers
- Nylon-jaw pliers
- Hot glue gun

1. Roll the edge of your ribbon over, add a thin line of glue and press to seal.

2. Fold over and glue once again.

3. Repeat steps 1 and 2 on the other end of your ribbon. Center your crimp on the ribbon edge. With a pair of nylon-jaw pliers, firmly close the crimp.

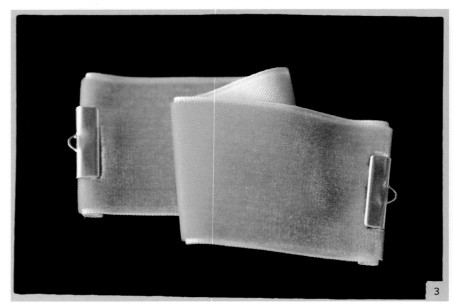

4. Attach three 9x6mm jump rings to one crimp, linking each to the other. Attach the lobster clasp to the other crimp with a 6mm jump ring. Lay out your embellishments and determine where you'd like everything set.

5. Attach your pin first, then sew on your flowers, starting from the back of the ribbon, through the center of the flower, bead and back. If you need to add a couple of stitches over the base of the flower petals to make them a little more secure, do it!

6. Push the rhinestone settings through from the rear of the ribbon, insert stones and push prongs down with the edge of the nylon-jaw pliers.

7. Aaah. A wee garden you don't have to water.

sash bracelet

Antique sash buckles are another curiosity that ends up in craft bins. Search for mother-of-pearl buckles on Etsy or eBay and you'll find loads of goodies to work with. You'll need to fit your ribbon to the slide opening—choose a width that's one and a half to two times the width of your slide opening to get a lush ruching effect and keep the pieces in place. Stiffer ribbons such as Petersham hold their shape beautifully.

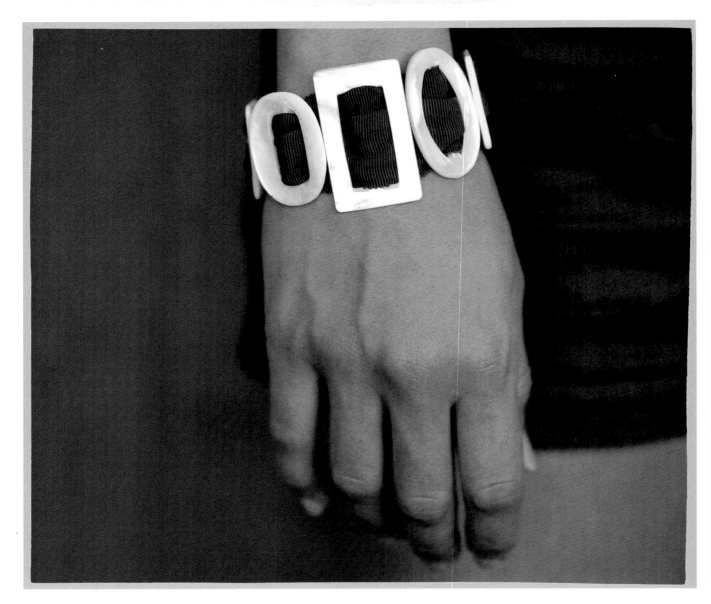

BITS YOU'LL NEED

- Mother-of-pearl sash slides/buckles (we used five varying 1½"–2" [3.8–5.1 cm] tall)
- 7" (17.8 cm) length of 2" (5.1 cm)-wide ribbon
- Two 19x5mm ribbon crimp ends
- Three 6mm jump rings, 16–18 gauge
- One 12x6mm lobster clasp

TOOLS

- Scissors
- Chain-nose pliers
- Flat-nose pliers
- Nylon-jaw pliers

1. Lay out your buckles in order.

2. Gather your ribbon and thread the buckles on one by one.

3. Arrange your buckles and fix any ribbon that is bunched up oddly. Try it on and trim your ribbon if necessary.

4. Gather your ribbon and softly pleat to fit the width of your ribbon crimp.

5. With a pair of nylon-jaw pliers, firmly close the crimp onto the ribbon.

6. Attach two jump rings to the crimp, linking each to the other.

7. Repeat steps 4 and 5 on the other end and attach the lobster clasp with the last jump ring.

8. Buckle up (sorry, couldn't help it).

concho bracelet

Just the right amount of Western, this bracelet will add a bit of awesome cowgirl to your look. You'll want ribbon that is a tad wider than the slide opening to help keep the conchos in place. Be sure to get ones with slots!

BITS YOU'LL NEED

• Conchos (we used six 1" [2.5 cm] round pieces with a ⅜" [1 cm] slot)
• 38" (96.5 cm) length of ribbon (we used ⅝" [1.6 cm] wide)

TOOLS

• Scissors
• Fray Check or clear nail polish

1. Fold your ribbon in half and thread the folded end through your first concho.

2. Continue adding the rest of your conchos, centering them on the ribbon.

3. Trim both ends of your ribbon and seal with Fray Check or clear nail polish. Pause, wait for it to dry and tie it on. Break out the cowboy boots for full effect.

shimmy shake Bracelet

Shimmering sequins are a demure way to add a dab of sparkle to your wrist. We used vintage French sequins we found on Etsy that have a slight aged patina, but there's nothing wrong with their contemporary cousins.

BITS YOU'LL NEED

- About fifty 5mm sequins
- Fifty (or more) 6x3mm jump rings, 18–22 gauge
- 7"–8" (17.8–20.3 cm) length of 2mm chain, cut to fit
- Two 4x3mm jump rings, 16–18 gauge
- One 9x6mm lobster clasp

TOOLS

- Chain-nose pliers
- Flat-nose pliers

1. Attach the lobster clasp to one end of your chain with a 4x3mm jump ring. Add the other 4x3mm ring to the opposite end.

2. Begin adding your sequins in the center of the chain with the 6x3mm jump rings.

3. Concentrate more sequins in the center of the chain, spacing them out gradually as you work toward the ends. Go glimmer.

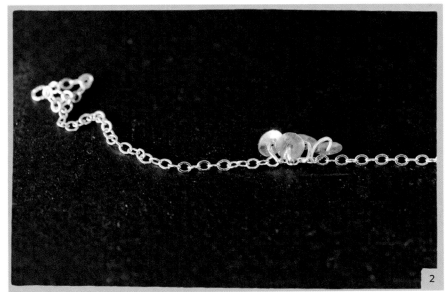

spike bracelet

Perfectly rock-and-roll, it's easy to understand why spikes are holding strong. Pair with classic denim and you're ready to well . . . you know.

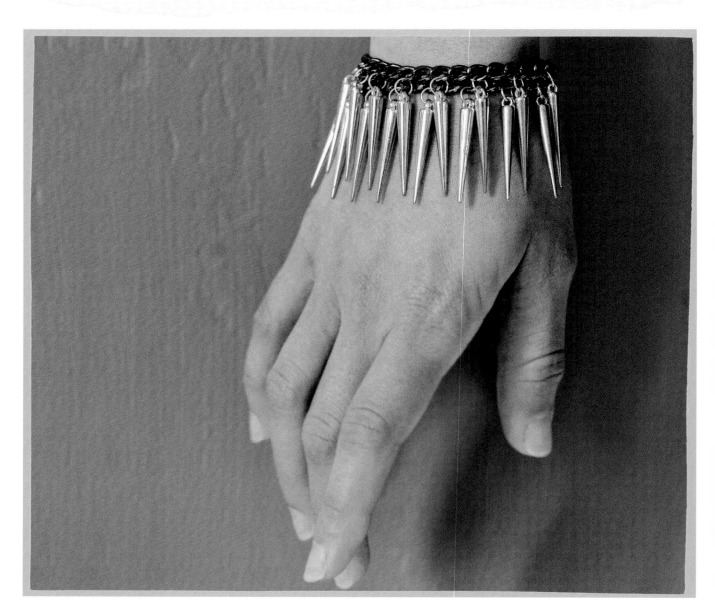

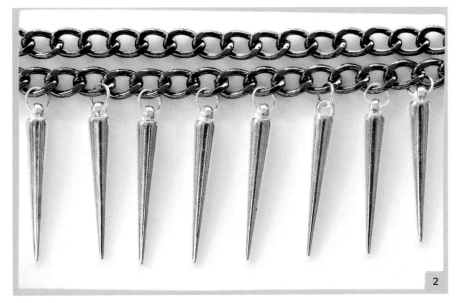

BITS YOU'LL NEED

- Eighteen (or more) 1½" (3.8 cm)-long silver spikes
- Two 6¼" (15.9 cm) lengths of 6–7mm gunmetal chain
- One 10x6mm gunmetal lobster clasp
- Eighteen (or more) 6mm silver jump rings, 16–18 gauge
- Four 9x6mm silver jump rings, 16–18 gauge

TOOLS

- Chain-nose pliers
- Flat-nose pliers

1. Link the two lengths of chain on each end with a 9x6mm jump ring. Ensure that chains are parallel and free of twists or kinks. Add two more jump rings to one end and a lobster clasp to the other.

2. Attach the spikes to one length of your chain at your desired intervals with 6mm jump rings. Be sure to link to the same side of the chain loops so they hang evenly.

3. Repeat step 2, adding spikes to the second length of chain.

4. Congrats on kicking up your street-style cred a notch.

chain

with so many variations to be found, this classic element of jewelry holds an appeal all its own. infused with meaning and purpose from its more tragic use in some of our darkest human times to aesthetic incarnations with sweeter symbolism, chain has endured the passing ages. from the opulently ornate to the daintily decorative or the indispensably industrial, there's something undeniably handsome and soothing about the rhythm of repetition and phenomenal function.

fringe cuff

Finished with flirty lengths of chain, a classic cuff is elevated from simple to showstopper. We used 2½- to 2¾-inch (6.4–7 cm) lengths of chain due to the curve of our cuff, spacing the drill holes 3 mm apart. If you are using a larger cuff, you'll need to do a little math to figure out how many jump rings and how much chain is required.

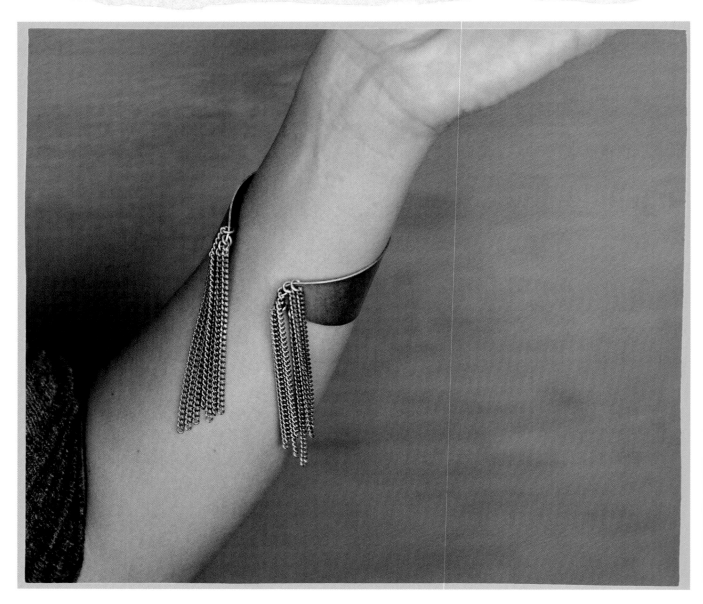

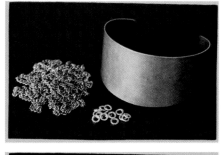

BITS YOU'LL NEED

- One brass cuff (ours is 1½" [3.8 cm] tall in the middle and about ½" [1.3 cm] tall near the ends)
- 35" (89 cm) length of 3mm brass curb chain
- Fourteen 5mm jump rings, 16–18 gauge

TOOLS

- Metal shears
- Chain-nose pliers
- Flat-nose pliers
- Drill
- #52 drill bit
- Safety glasses
- Marker

1. With a permanent marker, mark your drill holes on both sides.

2. Drill holes.

3. Cut your first length of chain and attach it to the center with a 5mm jump ring. We started with a 2½-inch (5.1 cm) piece.

4. Attach your full length of chain to the next hole. Since our cuff is tapered, we held it level and trimmed the chain after it was attached, so all the ends lined up.

5. Continue adding your chain, trimming each length after you've attached it.

6. Repeat steps 3–5 on the other side.

the skinny Handpiece

Unbelievably easy to whip up, this sleek little something is a perfectly delicate touch. If you're feeling fancy, you can dress up the connection point with a pretty focal or charm.

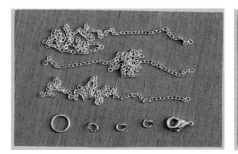

BITS YOU'LL NEED

- Three 3x4mm jump rings, 18–22 gauge
- One 8mm jump ring, 16–18 gauge
- One 10x6mm lobster clasp
- Two 6½" (16.5 cm) lengths of 1–2mm chain
- 7" (17.8 cm) length of 1–2mm chain

TOOLS

- Chain-nose pliers
- Flat-nose pliers

1. Link both ends of the 7" (17.8 cm) chain to a 3x4mm jump ring, making sure there are no twists or kinks.

2. Connect the two 6½" (16.5 cm) chains to the same jump ring as shown.

3. Link the lobster clasp to one free end with a 3x4mm jump ring, and link an 8mm jump ring to the other end with your last 3x4mm jump ring.

4. You can wear it now. No, seriously, that's it.

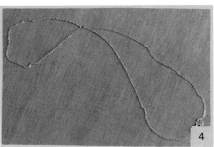

tangled bracelet

This is a great use for all the scraps of chain and damaged pieces that inevitably pile up; you can also purchase chain to supplement your piece if you're not a I'll-use-it-someday hoarder like we are. We cut lengths down from larger strands, but also linked up shorter scraps for a piece that embodies a mix of neglected jewel box and city-street cool. Our chain averaged 3 mm wide, so if you are using chunkier chains you'll need fewer strands.

BITS YOU'LL NEED

- Lots of chain, varying styles and textures (we used about sixty-four 6¼" [15.9 cm] strands)
- Five 8mm jump rings, 14–16 gauge
- One 12mm jump ring, 12–16 gauge
- Sixteen 6x4mm jump rings, 18 gauge
- One 24x15mm lobster clasp

TOOLS

- Metal shears
- Chain-nose pliers
- Flat-nose pliers

1. Cut and assemble (if linking from small scraps) your chain lengths.

2. Divide chains into eight groups—they don't have to have the same number of chains each, but rather be visually balanced. Link each chain group to a 6x4mm jump ring. Repeat on the opposite end. Set aside four of these eight connected groups; you'll be working with four chain bundles at a time.

3. Link all four groups to an 8mm jump ring on one end.

4. Loosely twist two of the chain groups together.

5. And then the other two.

6. Join the free ends of the twisted lengths to another 8mm jump ring.

7. Repeat with the other four groups of chain.

8. Join your two new clusters to a 12mm jump ring.

9. On the opposite end, connect the two clusters to a lobster clasp with an 8mm jump ring.

10. Oh, what a tangled tactile treat!

Hammered Link Bracelet

Brass links make a great base for further embellishment. Add gemstone drops or rustic charms and even play with the shape, size and arrangement of the links for new variations.

BITS YOU'LL NEED
- 16-gauge brass wire
- Template (page 212)

TOOLS
- Metal shears or wire snips
- Round-nose pliers
- Hammer
- Steel bench block
- Suede sandbag (optional)
- File

1. Cut a 1-inch (2.5 cm) piece of wire for your first link.

2. With round-nose pliers, shape your wire into a ¾-inch (1.9 cm) circle, overlapping by ¼ inch (6 mm).

3. Hammer. You should be able to open your link with a little effort, but it should not slip open easily.

4. Repeat steps 1–3, joining your links as you go until your desired length is achieved.

5. Using the hammered link template, bend your wire to match and hammer flat.

6. Attach the hook to the last link of your bracelet by opening link and slipping on.

7. You made it!

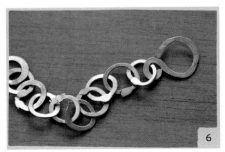

silver Lining Bracelet

Make your own chains with little links and connectors, then mix them up with premade chain for a subtle textural statement.

BITS YOU'LL NEED

• Two 8mm silver-plated jump rings, 16–18 gauge
• Ten 5mm silver-plated jump rings, 16–18 gauge
• Twenty-four 6x3mm silver-plated jump rings, 18–20 gauge
• One five-strand silver-plated D-ring toggle clasp
• Two 5" (12.7 cm) lengths of silver-plated chain
• Silver links/connectors (enough to make three 5" [12.7 cm] lengths when connected)

TOOLS

• Chain-nose pliers
• Flat-nose pliers

1. Set the order your strands will go in and lay out your links to length.

2. With a 5mm jump ring, begin connecting your chain to the clasp.

3. With a 5mm jump ring, connect your first link to the clasp.

4. Continue connecting the links together with 6x3mm jump rings.

5. Repeat for each new chain strand. When all your pieces are linked, connect them to the opposite clasp with 5mm jump rings.

6. Connect the toggle bar to the clasp with two 8mm jump rings, linking each to the other.

7. Next project, please.

fabric + cord

oh textiles and trim, how i love you and your many varied looks. whether i'm feeling soft and femme, crisp and tailored (rare, but it happens), rugged and rustic, vibrantly vintage or kitsch to the max—you always have my back. thank you for giving us so many opportunities to play dress-up.

doily cuff

A metallic coat imparts a lavish twist on classic crochet. Just what your little black dress is missing. A thicker cotton doily works best for this project. Choose one that is small enough to wrap almost all the way around your wrist, leaving a 1- to 1½-inch (2.5–3.8 cm) gap at the rear.

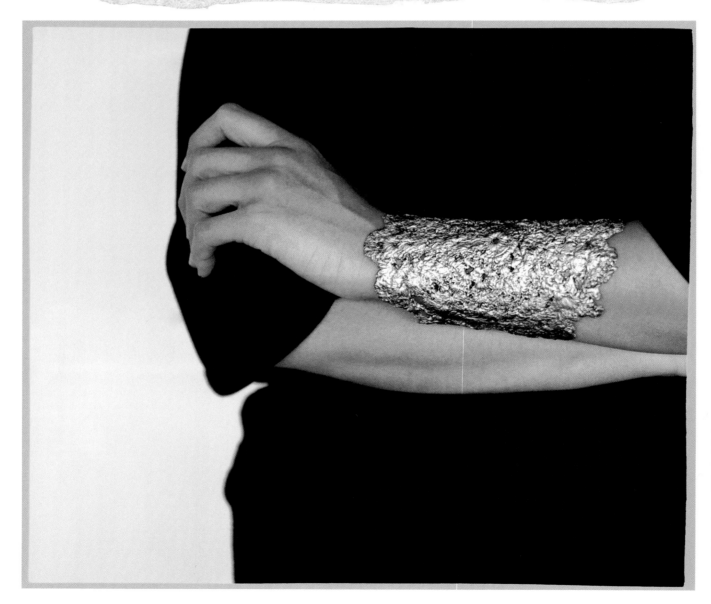

1–2

3

4

BITS YOU'LL NEED

- Doily (5½" [14 cm] in diameter)
- Fabric stiffener
- Gilding size
- Gold leafing sheets
- Clear acrylic spray
- Black acrylic paint (to antique, if desired)
- Needle and thread
- Three 5mm jump rings, 16–18 gauge
- 3"–4" (7.6–10.2 cm) of 4–5mm chain (something that is easily grasped by your clasp)
- One 12x9mm lobster clasp

TOOLS

- Bottle or can (about the size of your wrist)
- Measuring tape
- Tapered chisel brush (about 1" [2.5 cm] wide)
- Sponge brush (about 1" [2.5 cm] wide)
- Gilder's mop (soft fluffy brush)
- Foil/pastic wrap

1. Check your mold measurement (you'll want something about the size of your wrist) and prepare your mold. If you are using something fiber based, wrap it in foil or plastic wrap first so your doily will not stick.

2. Dip the doily in fabric stiffener, allowing it to absorb while working it into the fabric.

3. Drape over your mold. Secure the edges by running a thread through and tying off.

4. Allow to dry overnight. If you are in a humid environment, you may need an extra day. You can also speed drying with a hair dryer.

5. Once it is fully cured, apply size with a sponge brush.

6. When size is dried, but still tacky, press your gold leaf down (paper side up) and use a tapered chisel brush to push the leaf into the nooks and crannies. Carefully pull the sheet away, working slowly to prevent tears. Continue until entire piece is covered.

7. You'll likely have excess leaf hanging from the cuff after applying. Dust these off with a gilder's mop.

8. Apply two or three coats of a clear acrylic spray, following manufacturer's instructions for drying time between coats.

9. If you want an antiqued look, gingerly sponge a tiny bit of black acrylic paint onto your piece, working into crevices, and wipe off excess with a paper towel or cloth.

10. Attach the clasp on one end with two 5mm jump rings. Attach chain on other end with a 5mm jump ring. Trim chain to fit.

11. Now you're ready to outshine them all.

MIDAS ROPE BRACELET

A simple reef knot is elevated to excellent by twisty lengths of gilt trim.

BITS YOU'LL NEED

- Two 8" (20.3 cm) lengths of ⅜" (1 cm) metallic gold cord trim
- Two 2" (5.1 cm) pieces of wire, 24 gauge
- Two 10x5mm ribbon crimp ends
- One 12mm toggle clasp
- Two 4x6mm jump rings, 18 gauge
- One 5mm jump ring, 18 gauge

TOOLS

- Scissors
- Chain-nose pliers
- Flat-nose pliers
- Nylon-jaw pliers

1. Bend your cords in half and loop to make a loose reef knot.

2. Pull taut.

3. Test the length and check your fit. You'll be trimming the cord and crimping it just over the spot you wrap with a length of wire. You should have about a 1-inch (2.5 cm) gap between the cord ends when bracelet is seated comfortably on your wrist. Loop a length of wire around and twist taut with a pair of pliers.

4. Trim wire and bend flat against cord. Trim cord.

5. You may need to widen your crimp to get it over the cord. Do this by inserting and opening your flat-nose pliers on the interior.

6. Center the ribbon crimp on the cord, covering the wire. With a pair of nylon-jaw pliers, firmly close the crimp.

7. Attach the toggle loop with a 5mm jump ring. Attach the toggle bar to the other end with two 4x6mm jump rings, linking each to the other.

8. You're totally golden.

Bouquet Bracelet

Thoroughly feminine, metallic beads add a hint of shine to a delicate landscape. These look beautiful stacked in complementary colors.

BITS YOU'LL NEED

- 7" (17.8 cm) length of ½" (1.3 cm) woven floral trim (longer for larger wrists)
- Twelve (or more) 2.5mm metallic beads (extra is good, because they like to fall and hide at your feet)
- Two 6x5mm ribbon crimp ends
- One 10x6mm lobster clasp
- Three 4x6mm jump rings, 18 gauge
- Thread to match trim

TOOLS

- Scissors
- Chain-nose pliers
- Flat-nose pliers
- Nylon-jaw pliers
- Needle

1. Check your fit and cut your trim as necessary. There should be a ½-inch (1.3 cm) gap between the trim ends when wrapped comfortably about wrist. Center the ribbon crimp on the trim. With a pair of nylon-jaw pliers, firmly close the crimp. Attach the clasp with one jump ring. Attach the remaining two jump rings to the other end, linking each to the other.

2. Threading your needle from the rear of the piece, sew on your beads. Two stitches through the center should be sufficient.

3. Continue stitching all of your beads on one by one.

4. Sew pretty (you saw that one coming, no?).

knotty sailor bracelet

Feeling landlocked? Knot your way to a nautical look. Quick snaps and rings are available at your local hardware store. You can substitute a ¾- to 1-inch (1.9–2.5 cm) D-ring if you can't find a round one.

BITS YOU'LL NEED

- Four 16" (40.6 cm) lengths of ⅜" (1 cm) woven cotton cord or rope
- One skein of embroidery floss
- One ⅝" (1.6 cm) brass rigid round eye quick snap
- One 1" (2.5 cm) brass ring
- 8" (20.3 cm) length of scrap twine/cord
- G-S Hypo Fabric Cement

TOOLS

- Scissors
- Hot glue gun

1. With two cords, make a loop.

2. Weave your other two cords through the first loop.

3. Pull taut and fix any twists or overlap in the cords.

4. Thread four of the cords on one side through the eye of the snap.

5. Facing the snap opening up, fold the cords back onto themselves to fit. Tie with a piece of scrap cord or twine to hold in position.

6. Measuring against your wrist, thread the ring onto the second set of ropes on the opposite side, and fold them onto themselves. Tie with a piece of scrap cord or string to hold in position.

7. Check your fit. Snap should easily hook onto your ring. Adjust if you need to.

8. Lift the ropes on one side a bit and dab with a little hot glue. Press and hold to seal.

9. Remove your tie.

10. Begin whipping. See techniques (page 211) for detail.

11. Trim cords. Dab ends with fabric cement.

12. Repeat steps 8–11 on the opposite side.

13. Style ho!

Tassel Bracelet

Playful tassels lend both textural appeal and a splash of color to this easy-breezy bracelet. Play with color and size. Make your tassels longer, shorter, all even or mixed lengths. We've clustered three here, but you can make more and load up all 360 degrees of chain for a mega statement piece.

BITS YOU'LL NEED

- Three skeins of embroidery floss in coordinating colors
- G-S Hypo Fabric Cement
- 6"–7" (15.2–17.8 cm) length of chain
- Two 7mm jump rings, 16–18 gauge
- One 10mm jump ring, 16 gauge
- One 19x11mm lobster clasp
- One 13mm jump ring, 14–16 gauge

TOOLS

- Scissors
- Flat-nose pliers
- Chain-nose pliers
- Cardstock (an old business card works great!)

1. Cut a piece of card 2 inches (5.1 cm) wide. Begin wrapping your floss around.

2. Wrap twenty-five to forty times around, until you're happy with the plushness of your tassel. Trim. Take a separate length of floss, measure out 3 inches (7.6 cm), then fold back and forth until it is four strands thick. Trim.

3. Gather the folded strand and pull through your tassel wrap.

4. Tie in a knot and dab a little fabric cement on the knot.

5. Move the knot under the tassel.

6. Holding the tassel threads together, slip it off the card.

7. Begin whipping the tassel (see techniques, page 211).

8. Cut the bottom loops and trim the tassel end.

9. Repeat steps 1–8 to make two more tassels. If you'd like one to be a bit shorter, simply trim it to length.

10. Hang all three tassels on a 13mm jump ring. Measure and separate your chain into two lengths. Connect the jump ring with tassels in the center of two chain lengths. Attach the clasp to one end with a 7mm jump ring, and the 10mm jump ring to the other end, linking with a 7mm jump ring.

11. Wear.

coupled bracelet

Just the right amount of rugged, copper hardware gives an industrial polish to hemp rope. We've listed material dimensions for two versions, one brawnier than the other.

BITS YOU'LL NEED
(FOR LARGE VERSION)

- One ½" x ½" (1.3 x 1.3 cm) copper slip coupling
- Three 8" (20.3 cm) lengths of 6mm hemp rope

(FOR SMALL VERSION)

- Two 8" (20.3 cm) lengths of 3mm hemp rope
- 8" (20.3 cm) length of 6mm hemp rope
- One ⅜" x ⅜" (1 cm) copper slip coupling

TOOLS

- Scissors
- Hot glue gun

1. Tape your rope before cutting so the ends don't fray. Dab a bit of hot glue on the cut ends to seal them up.

2. With hot glue, stick the three ends together so that they're connected for about a 1-inch (2.5 cm) length. Repeat on the opposite end.

3. With your coupling within reach, bead a ring of glue ¼ inch (6 mm) from the end of your joined ropes.

4. Quickly insert into the coupling with a twisting motion, until rope ends are halfway in.

5. Repeat the process on the other end, first adding extra glue inside the coupling.

6. Quickly apply a bead of glue around the ropes ¼ inch (6 mm) from the end and insert into coupling with a twisting motion.

7. Allow the glue to cool for a few minutes before trying on.

lace cuff

New or repurposed, lace of any sort makes a pretty piece. We picked vintage and antique metallic weaves to give this ladylike bracelet a little edge and a good pop of glam.

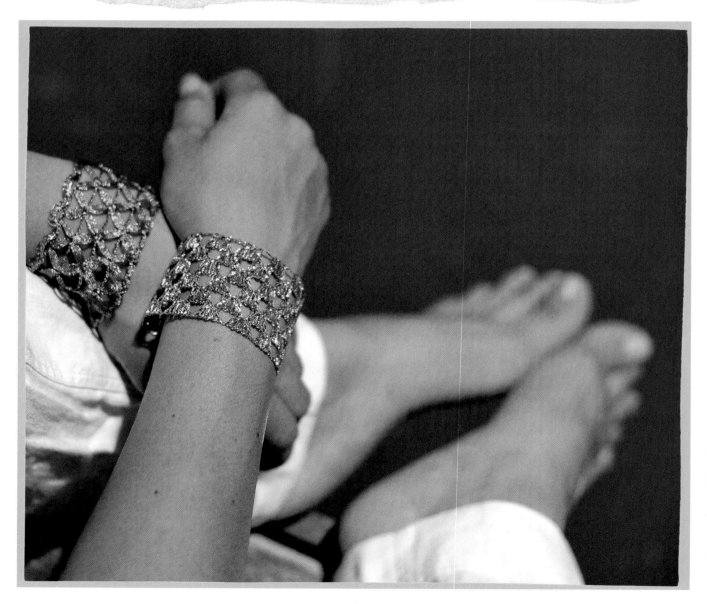

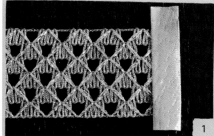

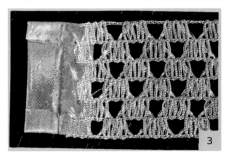

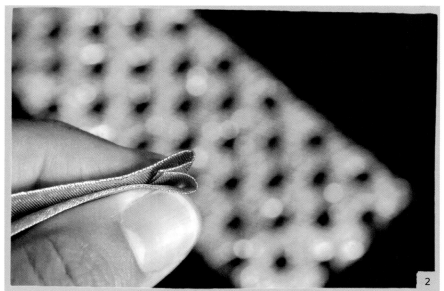

BITS YOU'LL NEED

- Two 7" (17.8 cm) lengths of lace ribbon (we used 2¼" [5.7 cm]-wide ribbon)
- Bias tape
- Four 19x5mm ribbon crimp ends
- Two 4x6mm jump rings, 18 gauge
- Two 10mm jump rings, 18 gauge
- Two 12x6mm lobster clasps

TOOLS

- Scissors
- Chain-nose pliers
- Flat-nose pliers
- Nylon-jaw pliers
- Hot glue gun

1. Big wrist? Small wrist? Wrap ribbon around your wrist so it is slightly loose. Trim so there is about a ½-inch (1.3 cm) gap between the ends. Cut your bias tape about ½ inch (1.3 cm) longer than your ribbon width.

2. Fold the excess bias tape into itself and crease. Do this on the top and bottom edge.

3. Since you'll be using HOT glue, take care not to burn yourself. Press any edges down with a piece of card or a spoon rather than your fingers unless you don't mind a blister or three. Now that we are clear on that, with a few dots of hot glue, stick the top and bottom folds down. Sandwich your ribbon edge in between the folds of the bias tape. Apply a few small dots of glue and fold and press (again with a card or something without nerves) the bias tape over the ribbon.

4. Center the ribbon crimp on the bias tape. With a pair of nylon-jaw pliers, firmly close the crimp onto the ribbon. Attach a 10mm jump ring to one end. Attach the lobster clasp with a 4x6mm jump ring to the opposite end.

5. Make another. That way one wrist won't be jealous.

ferrule bracelet

Understated brass hardware gives soft silk a warm touch. You can find brass ferrules (sometimes called compression rings) at your local hardware store. If you pick smaller or larger ferrules, test them out in the store—the three center ferrules should not be able to slide over the end ferrules.

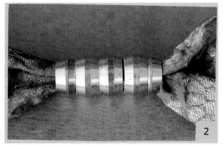

BITS YOU'LL NEED

- Three ⁷⁄₁₆" (1.1 cm) brass ferrules
- Two ⁵⁄₁₆" (8 mm) brass ferrules
- 9" (22.9 cm) length of fabric, 4"–5" (10.2–12.7 cm) wide
- Two 19x5mm ribbon crimp ends
- Three 5mm jump rings, 18 gauge
- One 12mm toggle clasp

TOOLS

- Scissors
- Chain-nose pliers
- Flat-nose pliers
- Nylon-jaw pliers
- Hot glue gun

1. Bunch your fabric together and slide a ⁷⁄₁₆-inch (1.1 cm) ferrule onto the center. Play with your fabric, arranging it so any frayed ends are rolled and tucked out of sight.

2. Continue adding your ferrules, placing one ⁵⁄₁₆-inch (8 mm) ferrule on each end of the three ⁷⁄₁₆-inch (1.1 cm) ones.

3. Trim your fabric on each end to fit. There should be about a ½-inch (1.3 cm) gap between the two ends when bracelet is comfortably wrapped on your wrist.

4. Shape your fabric and gather an end.

5. Insert into crimp, making sure no fabric is bleeding out on the sides.

6. Crimp closed with a pair of nylon-jaw pliers. Repeat on the other end.

7. Attach the toggle loop with a 5mm jump ring. Attach the toggle bar to the other end with two 5mm jump rings, linking each to the other.

8. Finish arranging fabric. If necessary, add a bit of glue to the interior seams to keep in place.

bohemian wrap bracelet

Golden brass adds a warm touch to graphic blocks of color. Pick your favorite hues and wrap away.

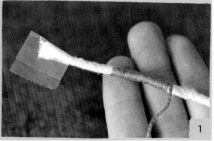

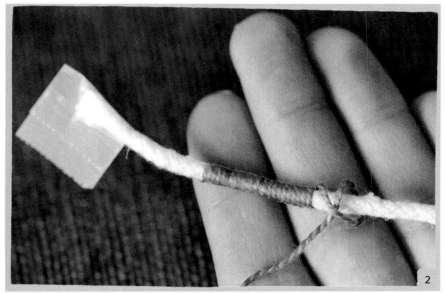

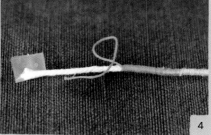

BITS YOU'LL NEED

- 2" x 2" (5.1 x 5.1 cm) brass sheet, 28 gauge
- Four skeins of embroidery floss
- 9" (22.9 cm) length of ⅜" (1 cm) woven cotton cord or rope
- Fray Check
- E6000 adhesive
- Two glue-in cord ends with loop, 9 mm inside diameter
- Two 7mm jump rings, 16–18 gauge
- One 10mm jump ring, 16 gauge
- One 12x9mm lobster clasp

TOOLS

- Scissors
- Metal shears
- Sandpaper
- Flat-nose pliers
- Round-nose pliers

1. Tape the ends of your rope to prevent fraying. About 1 inch (2.5 cm) from the end, begin wrapping with floss, burying a ½-inch (1.3 cm) piece and wrapping over it. Keep your wrapping close and tight.

2. When you've wrapped about 1 inch (2.5 cm), loop the working end under the last strand, pull and lay against rope.

3. Using your second color, bury the end once again and tightly wrap over the buried ends of both colors.

4. Repeat step 3, alternating colors as you please until you've wrapped a bit over 6 inches (15.2 cm) of your cord.

5. When wrapping your last color block, whip the floss (see techniques, page 211). Working all the way around, soak a little Fray Check into the last ⅛ inch (3 mm) of the colored ends and ⅛ inch (3 mm) of the naked cord below.

6. Set aside and let dry. Get your brass sheet out. With the metal shears, cut eight strips measuring ¼ x ¾ inch (6 mm x 1.9 cm).

7. Sand edges.

8. Using round-nose pliers, curl the metal strips into a C shape. Make sure they are even and not tapered.

9. Slip a metal strip onto the wrapped cord; the curve should fit without any room for movement. Continue to curl around, squeezing with flat-nose pliers as you rotate.

10. Continue adding metal curls at random intervals until you're happy with the arrangement.

11. Once Fray Check is dry, cut the cord with a little bleed from your wrap.

12. Glue into cord ends with E6000 and allow to dry, following manufacturer's instructions.

13. Once the glue has cured, attach the lobster clasp to one end with a 7mm jump ring and the 10mm to the other, linking with a 7mm jump ring.

14. Peruse the book and find this bracelet a buddy to make next.

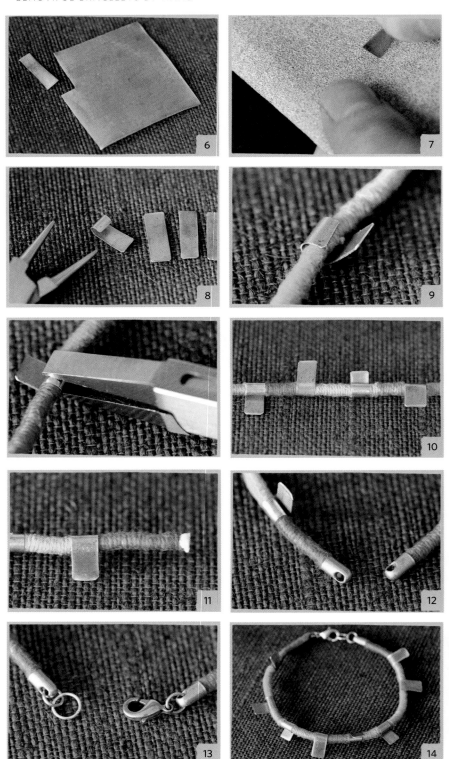

Bauble wrap Bangle

Sparkle and a classic shirt pattern collide for a mishmash of prep and glam, while frayed edges add a rock-star touch. Remainder bins at fabric stores are a great place to pick up small pieces of material. Stalking a male friend's closet for shirts that are past their prime is a good way to go, too.

BITS YOU'LL NEED

- One wood bangle, about ½"–¾" (1.3–1.9 cm) wide
- Two rhinestone buttons with shanks, ¾" and 1" (1.9 and 2.5 cm) diameter
- 1 yard of fabric, 2"–3" (5.1–7.6 cm) wide (ripped down for a frayed edge instead of cut)
- 26-gauge wire

TOOLS

- Scissors
- Flat-nose pliers
- Drill
- Drill bit (slightly larger than shank width)
- Safety glasses
- Hot glue gun

1. Measure the width and thickness of your button shanks.

2. You'll be drilling a slot into the bangle to insert the shank into.

3. Mark off your width and thickness and drill your opening. You can make several small holes, then wiggle the bit between them to open up into one large space.

4. Test the fit of your button; it should slide in easily, with a tiny bit of extra room. If the fit is too tight, don't force it or you may crack the bangle or the shank. Just use the drill to open it up a bit more.

5. Position your second button and repeat steps 3 and 4.

6. Remove both buttons. Depending on your bangle thickness, lace a 6- to 10-inch (15.2–25.4 cm) length of wire through a shank, centering the button on the wire. Bend the ends together and make a small twist to secure at the base of the shank. Repeat for second button.

7. Insert the buttons back into their slots. Again, if it is too tight, drill it out a little to accommodate the added wire.

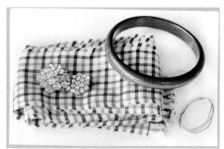

8. Loop the wire around the bangle twice until both ends meet. Twist with a pair of pliers to secure. Bend back any extra wire so it lies flush with the bangle surface.

9. Cut a slight taper at the first end of your fabric (to fit between buttons).

10. Dab a spot of glue on the inside of your bangle, behind the buttons, and press your fabric on to adhere. Thread it around and between the buttons.

11. Wrap the fabric around tightly, adding a drop of glue on the interior of the bangle every few wraps.

12. When you get back around to the button, wrap around the back and trim so there is just enough fabric to fit between the center of the buttons.

13. Dab a bit of glue on the end of your fabric and push it in between the buttons, pressing down to secure. And you're done!

Fat Eighth Bracelet

I'm not a quilter by any means, but I still can't resist picking up bundles of quilting fabric. You can also substitute fabric remainders or even a cool vintage scarf—the quick and simple assembly will have you yearning to make multiples. If you want a less tailored look, skip the fusible tape and let the raw edges show.

BITS YOU'LL NEED
- One fat eighth
- ¼" EZ-Steam II fusible tape
- Two 19x5mm ribbon crimp ends
- One 4x6mm jump ring, 18 gauge
- One 10mm jump ring, 18 gauge
- One 12x6mm lobster clasp

TOOLS
- Scissors
- Iron
- Nylon-jaw pliers
- Chain-nose pliers
- Flat-nose pliers

1. Iron your fabric to get rid of any wrinkles or creases.

2. Working along the long edge, fold and iron a ½-inch (1.3 cm) edge.

3. Apply a strip of fusible tape along the inside of your fold. Follow manufacturer's instructions to fuse.

4. Repeat on the other long edge.

5. Fold both edges of your fabric to meet in the center.

6. Overlap one edge so it covers the bottom edge slightly wider than your fusible tape. Apply a strip of tape underneath and follow manufacturer's instructions to fuse.

7. You should now have a nice tube of fabric. Knot loosely in the middle, keeping seam to the rear. Fuss with your knot until it looks just right.

8. Wrap around your wrist so it meets comfortably. Trim excess, leaving a ½-inch (1.3 cm) gap.

9. Gather one end of fabric, and pleat it onto itself to meet the width of your ribbon crimp.

10. Insert into ribbon crimp. With a pair of nylon-jaw pliers, firmly close the crimp onto the ribbon, making sure nothing is sticking out.

11. Repeat steps 9 and 10 on the other end. Attach a 10mm jump ring to one end, and the lobster clasp with a 4x6mm jump ring to the opposite end.

12. Supersimple, supersweet, *sí*?

knitted bracelet

Have old T-shirts you can rip to bits? Great. If not, you can easily buy fabric (and fabric loops!) at your local super-awesome fabric or craft shop. If you're using a white or natural fabric, try dip-dyeing to get an ombre effect. Is that trend still happening? Not sure why I'm asking, because I still love it anyway. You can link smaller strips together, so don't fret about having to find 60-inch (152.4 cm) lengths.

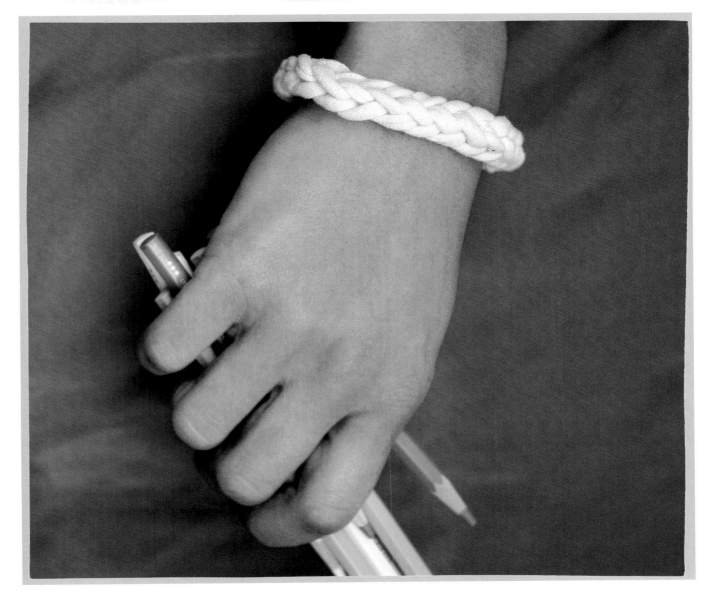

BITS YOU'LL NEED

• One 60" (152.4 cm) length of 1" (2.5 cm)-wide cotton knit jersey (with a bit of stretch)

TOOLS

• Scissors
• Your fingers (still attached)

1. If you need to connect strips to make a 60-inch (152.4 cm) length, cut ¼-inch (6 mm) slits ½ inch (1.3 cm) from each edge on all your pieces.

2. Overlap them.

3. Take the other end of your bottom strip and run it through the slits at the top.

4. Pull gently until you get a little knot.

5. Repeat until you have a 60-inch (152.4 cm) length.

6. Take one length and weave through fingers, leaving a 4-inch (10.2 cm) tail.

7. Take the long end and pull it behind your pinky and your ring finger. Weave over the top of your ring finger and then around the back of your pinky.

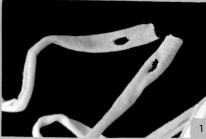

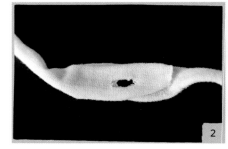

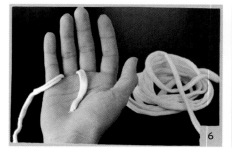

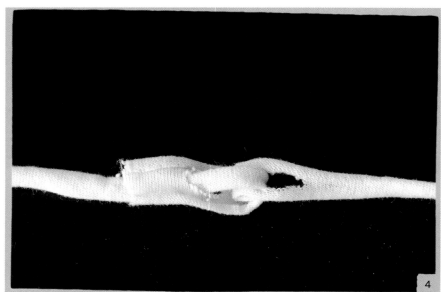

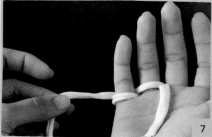

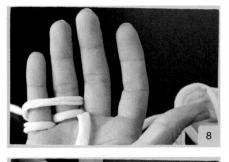

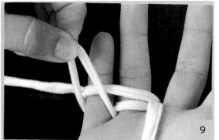

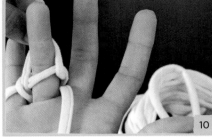

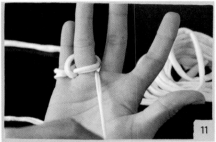

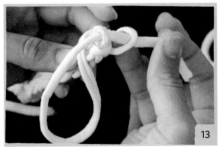

8. Bring the working end around the front of your pinky and ring finger.

9. Lift the loop on your pinky finger and slide over the top row and behind your finger.

10. Do the same with your ring finger.

11. Pull the working end across the two fingers again, and repeat steps 9 and 10. Keep pulling at the tail so the weave doesn't get too loose and is nice and neat.

12. When you've gotten to your desired length, pull the loops off your fingers, taking care to hold them securely. Slip the extra tail through both of the loops.

13. Pull all the way through, then knot your ends and tie a bow (or trim the ends neatly).

14. Get over how easy that was, and smile at any childhood flashbacks

Leather

Real or faux (vegan peeps, we have not forsaken you), leather adds just the right amount of tough luxe. Back in the day (ca. way-before-super-techno-fabric-and-down-filled-puffers-existed) our ancestors used leather to protect themselves from the elements. Durable, flexible and easy on the eyes, leather lets us take that bit for granted so we can lean on its aesthetic indulgences. Nothing wrong with that.

ball + chain wrap

An unexpected flash of metal against softly textured suede makes for a dynamic duo. You can easily play with the length, suede color and alternate metals for different looks.

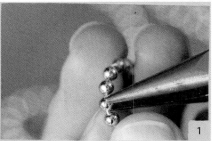

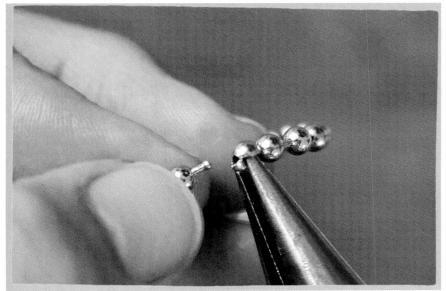

BITS YOU'LL NEED

- 29" (73.7 cm) length of 10x1.5mm suede lace (or faux suede)
- 29½" (74.9 cm) length of 3.2mm ball chain (you'll have a little overlap)
- Two 10x5mm ribbon crimp ends
- One 18x12mm lobster clasp
- Three 9mm round jump rings, 16-18 gauge
- Twenty-four (plus a few extra for mishaps) 5.5mm round jump rings, 20 gauge

TOOLS

- Scissors
- Nylon-jaw pliers
- Chain-nose pliers
- Flat-nose pliers

1. To separate the chain, align the edge of the pliers with the ball seam and apply pressure to crush and release the internal pin. You may need to use a second pair of pliers to pull the other half of the ball apart if the link does not release easily.

2. Align pin link of chain with end of suede lace.

3. Slide the open crimp end over both, taking care to keep the head of the link centered and underneath the teeth of the crimp end. Squeeze crimp end with nylon-jaw pliers until securely clamped.

4. Open a 5.5mm jump ring, slip over the front of the chain and tuck the suede into it (this will take a little patience) so that the jump ring is open on the rear side of the suede, away from the chain.

5. The first jump ring is spaced three ball links from the clasp. With the chain-and flat-nose pliers, wiggle the jump ring together until it is almost closed. With the chain-nose pliers, gently squeeze the jump ring until the ends overlap.

6. Rotate the piece and gently squeeze the jump ring from front to back to flatten the ends so they lie smooth.

7. Repeat steps 4–6, spacing the next twenty-two jump rings seven ball links apart. Space the final jump ring three ball links apart from the previous. Repeat step 1 to separate/trim the excess chain to match the length of the suede. Then repeat step 3 to finish the end.

8. Use a 5.5mm jump ring to attach the lobster claw to one crimp end. On the second end attach a 9mm jump ring, then add the other two 9mm jump rings, each to the previous.

9. Wrap it up!

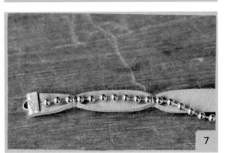

Hammered Circle with Leather Bracelet

Gold-printed black leather lends a big wink of wild animal to the subtle silhouette of this piece. Warm textured gold and a tiny pop of color make it perfect. If you can't find printed leather cord, you can easily touch up a plain piece with a bit of gold fabric paint using a pencil eraser as a stamp. If you'd prefer a shinier hammered finish, use a steel bench block.

BITS YOU'LL NEED

• Two 6" (15.2 cm) lengths of 4x1mm leather lace
• 12-gauge brass wire
• Thread

TOOLS

• Chain-nose pliers
• Flat-nose pliers
• Heavy-duty wire cutters
• Hammer
• File
• Needle

1. With the wire, make a circle a little over 1 inch (2.5 cm) in diameter. Overlap the wire by ½ inch (1.3 cm) and cut.

2. On a piece of concrete you don't care much about, gently hammer the wire until it has a slightly flattened face. Flip it over and hammer until it becomes slightly square. It should pick up the texture from the concrete.

3. With the chain-nose pliers, twist one end to form a little pocket for the other end of wire.

4. It should look like this.

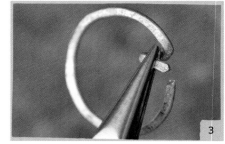

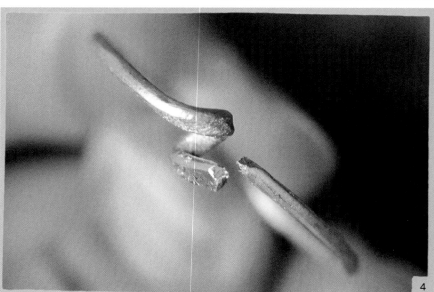

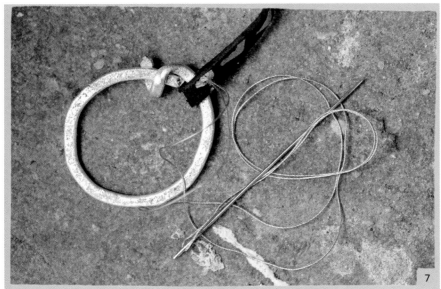

5. Squeeze the hoop so the wire fits into the twist. Squeeze with flat-nose pliers to secure.

6. Fold the leather over the hoop, leaving just enough to sew through comfortably.

7. Begin stitching from the middle. After a few stitches through both layers of leather, wrap around a few times before adding a final stitch to secure.

8. Repeat steps 6 and 7 with the second strip of leather.

9. *Grrrrr.*

Little Gem wrap

A crisp shot of hue adds a dignified sparkle to rustic suede. We splurged on fancy high-grade, double-drilled, emerald-cut iolite since the amount of beads used is so minimal, but don't lock yourself in. A single-hole bead will work just as well. To maintain the delicate feel of this piece, try to keep to beads under 6x6mm.

BITS YOU'LL NEED

- 1½" (3.8 cm) length of 6x4mm double-drilled beads
- 5" (12.7 cm) length of 3x1mm suede cord (faux or real)
- 20" (50 cm) length of 3x1mm suede cord (faux or real)
- Two 5mm jump rings, 18–20 gauge
- Five (or more) 6x4mm jump rings, 16–18 gauge
- One 11x7mm lobster clasp
- Two crimp bead covers
- Two 3x2mm crimp tubes
- 6" (15.2 cm) length of beading wire, 0.012" diameter (if your bead holes are larger, use a thicker wire)

TOOLS

- Scissors
- Crimping pliers
- Nylon-jaw pliers
- Chain-nose pliers
- Flat-nose pliers

1. Cut a 6-inch (15.2 cm) length of wire. Fold in half and string a crimp tube on, followed by beads. If you are using single-hole beads, do the same, but insert both wires through the single bead hole.

2. Run one length of suede through your loop.

3. Snuggle crimp up to lace and crimp closed with crimping pliers (see techniques, page 209).

4. Feed a crimp tube onto your free wires. Fold your other length of lace in half. Looping the wires around it, feed them back into the crimp tube and crimp closed.

5. Trim any excess wire. Using a pair of nylon-jaw pliers, cover crimp tubes with crimp bead covers.

6. Put a 5mm jump ring ¼ inch (6 mm) away from the edges of your lace.

7. With flat-nose pliers, squeeze the jump ring so it holds the laces firmly. Repeat on the other side.

8. Connect the lobster clasp with a 6x4mm jump ring.

9. Connect a series of 6x4mm jump rings on the other end to make your extender. We used four, but if you'd like a little more room to adjust, keep going.

10. Put on, look pretty.

Leather Feather Bracelet

Supple suede is easy to manipulate into fluttering feathers. Wear this to perk up denim for a look infused with a touch of Western luxe. Craft shops sell inexpensive bags of suede offcuts. Depending on the selection, you can mix more colors and layers in, or weed some out for a lighter feel.

BITS YOU'LL NEED

• Suede
• 7" (17.8 cm) length of chunky chain (ours is 9mm)
• Fourteen (or more) 7mm jump rings, 16–18 gauge
• Three 12mm jump rings, 14–16 gauge
• One 18x10mm lobster clasp
• Template (page 212)
• Fine-tip permanent marker

TOOLS

• Craft knife
• Cutting mat
• Chain-nose pliers
• Flat-nose pliers
• Leather punch

1. Add the clasp to one end of the chain with a 7mm jump ring.

2. Attach the three 12mm jump rings one by one to the other end of the chain, linking each to the other.

3. Lay out your suede and make a plan of attack. We made six small feathers and seven large ones (see template on page 212), but you may want more or less.

4. Copy the template and cut out along the outline.

5. Mark your suede and cut your feathers out with scissors or craft knife.

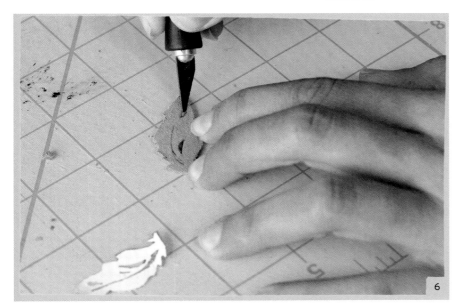

6. Make small detail cuts with a craft knife.

7. Punch holes at the top of all your pieces.

8. Beginning in the center and working outward, attach the large feathers to your chain with 7mm jump rings, ensuring there are adequate links in between for the small feathers. Attach the small feathers.

9. Well, hello you.

goldstone wrap bracelet

Gleaming goldstone mingles with dark leather, adding a demure dab of sparkle to the wrist. Look for a leather blank bracelet that wraps twice around your wrist.

BITS YOU'LL NEED

- One 23" (58.4 cm) blank leather wrap bracelet with closure
- 6" (15.2 cm) strand of goldstone beads, flat oval (about 14x10mm)
- 6" (15.2 cm) strand of goldstone beads, flat round (about 8mm)
- Two 9" (22.9 cm) lengths of beading wire, 0.024" diameter
- Four gold-plated crimp bead covers
- Four 3x2mm crimp tubes

TOOLS

- Scissors
- Crimping pliers
- Nylon-jaw pliers
- Chain-nose pliers
- Leather hole punch

1. Cut your bracelet blank in the middle.

2. Make two holes with the hole punch on each of the cut ends. Take care not to get too close to the edges. If you mess up, trim the leather back and try again.

3. Cut two 9-inch (22.9 cm) pieces of wire. Thread a crimp bead onto a wire, thread the wire through one hole, back through the crimp and close with crimping pliers. See techniques (page 209) for more detail. Repeat for the second hole.

4. Thread your beads onto each strand.

5. Working with one strand, thread a crimp bead on, thread the wire through a hole on the second half of the strap, through the crimp and close with crimping pliers.

6. Repeat step 5 on second strand.

7. Cover crimp tubes with crimp covers using nylon-jaw pliers. See techniques (page 209) for details.

orbit bracelet

Simple as can be, this is a great piece you can produce in many, many, many variations and a great gifting quickie. If you can tie a knot, you're pretty much in business. Looking to mix it up a little? Search for donuts in metal, gemstone, wood or shell and pair with coordinating cords.

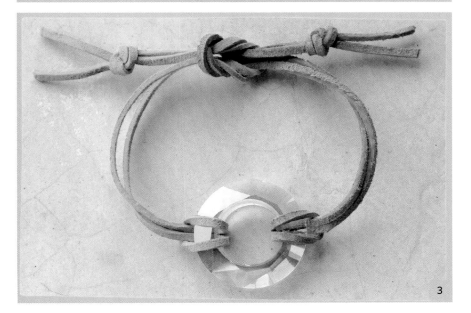

BITS YOU'LL NEED
- One glass donut focal (this one is 30mm)
- Two 16" (40.6 cm) lengths of 4x2mm suede (or faux suede) lace (we used aqua and lilac)

TOOLS
- Scissors

1. Fold a 16-inch (40.6 cm) length of lace in half and attach to the donut with a lark's head knot (see techniques, page 211).

2. Repeat with the second length of lace.

3. Tie an overhand knot 1 inch (2.5 cm) from each end (see techniques, page 211). Told you it was simple.

FIVE-strand suede braid bracelet

A ripe base for further embellishment, this saturated braid looks just fine mingling between metallic bangles and is ready to crash many an arm party.

BITS YOU'LL NEED

• Five 6" (15.2 cm) lengths of 4x1mm leather lace
• Two 19x5mm ribbon crimp ends
• Two 7x5mm jump rings, 18–20 gauge
• One 5mm jump ring, 16–18 gauge
• One 12x7mm lobster clasp

TOOLS

• Nylon-jaw pliers
• Chain-nose pliers
• Flat-nose pliers
• Scissors

1. With nylon-jaw pliers, crimp the ribbon end over your five strands of suede. Separate your strands so two are to the left and three to the right.

2. Bring the strand on the far right over to the center.

3. Bring the strand on the far left to the center and cross over the center strand.

4. That's it. Repeat steps 2 and 3 until you reach your desired length.

5. Trim and crimp with ribbon end.

6. Attach the lobster clasp with a 5mm ring and link two 7x5mm jump rings to the opposite end.

7. Well done.

metal

Used by ancient peoples as early as 6000 BCE, metals have long been coveted for their beauty and strength. Traditional techniques, fresh shapes and rustic handcrafted finishes blend beautifully in these projects for just-the-right-amount of modern appeal. Brass (a mixture of copper and zinc) and copper are inexpensive, easy to form and age beautifully, but they are easy enough to keep bright and polished if you wish. If you've got metal allergies, note that copper and most high-quality modern brass alloys (which I use in my own line) should not contain nickel, which is the irritating culprit. You might not have access to material data sheets and testing like we do, so if you're really worried you can seal your pieces with a clear acrylic spray or use sterling silver where possible. If using silver, I recommend practicing with brass first until you are confident in your techniques.

patina petal bracelet

Fluttering layers of petals drenched in color will pop perfectly against summer whites, bringing a dash of modern bohemian beauty to your look. Gilder's paste comes in a wide range of colors, so don't feel bound to use our favorite, green.

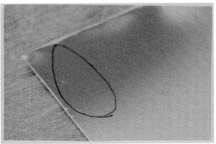

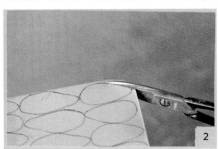

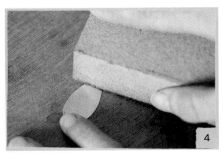

BITS YOU'LL NEED

- 5" x 5" (12.7 x 12.7 cm) 27-gauge brass sheet
- 7" (17.8 cm) length of brass chain
- One 12mm toggle clasp
- Two 4x3mm jump rings, 16–18 gauge
- Seventeen 6x4mm jump rings, 16–18 gauge
- Gilder's paste, patina
- Clear spray shellac or acrylic
- Template (page 212)
- Fine-tip permanent marker

TOOLS

- Metal shears (curved jaw preferably)
- Chain-nose pliers
- Flat-nose pliers
- Metal hole punch or drill
- File
- Sandpaper or sanding sponge
- Small piece of sponge cloth
- Paper towel

1. Using the template and a permanent marker, draw the outline of the shapes onto your sheet. Try to space them close together to conserve metal.

2. Cut with metal shears.

3. File and sand edges so no sharp portions remain.

4. Sand both sides of each petal to texture lightly—this will help the finish adhere a bit better.

5. Using your fingers, curve your petals.

6. Punch or drill holes at the top point of all your petals.

7. Working in a well-ventilated area, open your gilder's paste (it's a bit smelly). Pick up a bit of the paste on your piece of cloth or sponge (or your fingers) and dab onto both sides of your petals, holding them by the edge. When all your petals are coated, leave them to dry for an hour. Finish with three light coats of clear spray on both sides. Be sure to allow the pieces to dry in between coats.

8. Arrange the pieces and chain. Attach pieces to chain with 6x4mm jump rings, keeping links parallel so they hang evenly.

9. Attach the toggle to one end of the chain with two 4x3mm jump rings, linking each to the other. Attach the hoop to the other end with a 6x4mm jump ring.

10. Be impressed with yourself, you crafty thing, you.

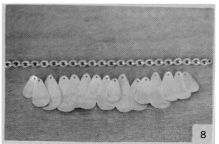

Fool's Gold Bangle

Chunky pyrite and subtly textured brass exude earthy elegance. If you want to give this piece some like company, try using the same formula with coordinating stones such as labradorite (or even cool old metal beads).

BITS YOU'LL NEED

• 7"–8" (17.8–20.3 cm) length of 12-gauge brass wire

• 3½"–4" (8.9–10.2 cm) length of 16-gauge brass wire

• 1½" (3.8 cm) length of pyrite beads (be sure they fit on 12-gauge wire, or scale your wire gauge down just a bit)

TOOLS

• Round-nose pliers

• Flat-nose pliers

• Heavy-duty wire cutters

• Hammer

• Steel bench block

• Suede sandbag (optional)

• File

1. File the ends of your wire flat.

2. Starting at one end of the 12-gauge wire, hammer it from end to end. It should bend and curve a bit, but not twist.

3. String your beads onto the 16-gauge wire.

4. Hammer the ends of the 16-gauge wire so they are slightly spatulate.

5. With round-nose pliers, begin making a loop. Make sure it is big enough to fit over the end of your large wire.

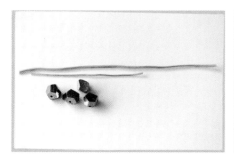

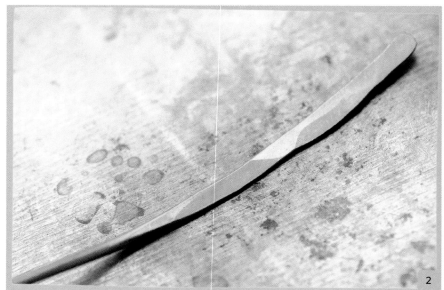

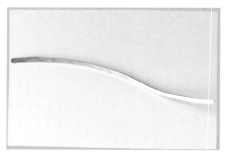

6. With flat-nose pliers, grab the end of the wire and wrap around until flush with stem. Repeat on the other side.

7. With your fingers, shape the large wire—shape the long into a U-shape to fit your wrist. Curve one end of the large wire, leaving enough of a gap to slide the wire loop over. Curve the other end less, creating a slight hook.

8. Slip the wire with the beads over the almost-closed curve.

9. There should be some tension in the larger wire that requires you to bend it to slip the other loop on. If there isn't (or if there is too much), gently shape the wire with your hands until just right. Slip the large wire through the other loop.

10. Using the round-nose pliers, close the hooked end to match the opposite side. *Fini!*

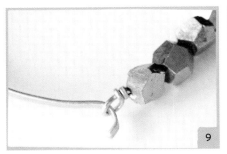

geometry Bangles

A minimalist delight of simple shapes highlighted with gritty texture makes for an instant favorite. If you'd prefer a shinier hammered finish, use a steel bench block.

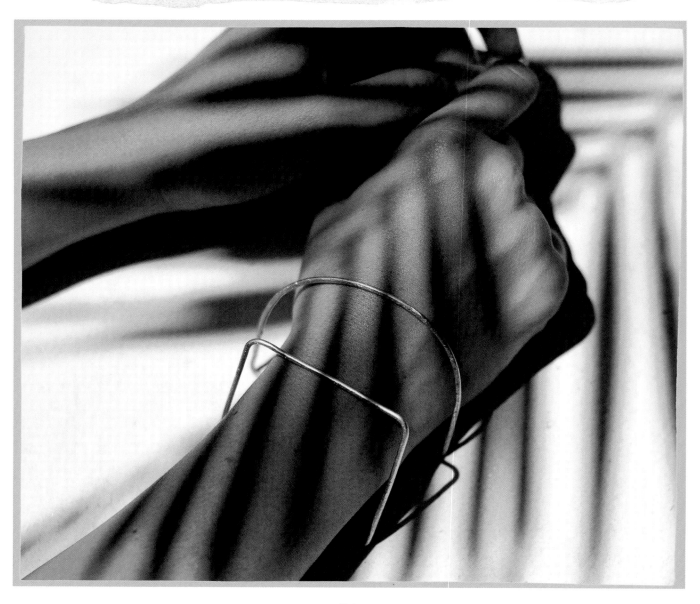

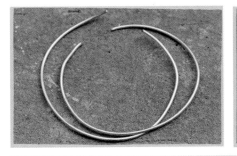
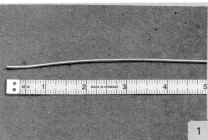

BITS YOU'LL NEED
• 9½" (24.1 cm) length of 12-gauge brass wire
• 10" (25.4 cm) length of 12-gauge brass wire

TOOLS
• Flat-nose pliers
• Heavy-duty wire cutters
• Hammer
• File

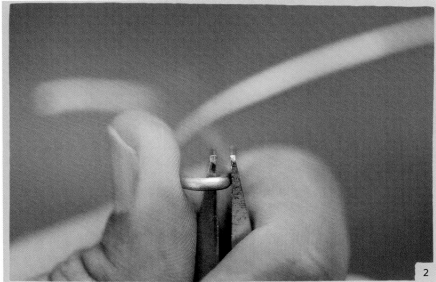

1. Measure your wire. You'll need about 9½ inches (24.1 cm) for the half round bangle that we are starting with.

2. For the half round bangle, make your first bend 3¾ inches (9.5 cm) away from an edge. Use a pair of flat-nose pliers and bend, until wire ends cross over. This will help work harden the metal and preserve your shape.

3. With your hands, pull wires back apart until you have a right angle.

4. Using the flat-nose pliers, gently squeeze and work out any massively bumpy bits. Straighten out the 3¾-inch (9.5 cm) length.

5. Make another bend along the straightened length, ¾ inch (1.9 cm) from the wire end. With your fingers, curve the remaining length of wire into a semicircle until it meets end to end.

6. File the ends of your wire flat.

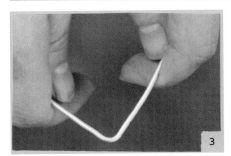

7. Wiggle the piece until the wire ends meet.

8. On a piece of concrete you don't care much about, gently hammer the wire until it has a slightly flattened face. Flip it over and hammer until it becomes slightly square. It should pick up the texture from the concrete. If the edges moved while you were hammering, work back into shape and file the ends again if necessary.

9. For the square bangle, measure and cut a 10-inch (25.4 cm) length of wire. Repeat the same bending and shaping process, making your first bend ½ inch (1.3 cm) from the wire end, then 2¼ inches (5.7 cm) from that three more times. Don't trust the ruler too much—eyeball it to make sure it actually looks square.

10. You should have a little overlap when you come to the end.

11. Trim and file so the edges meet.

12. Repeat step 8. Eight is great!

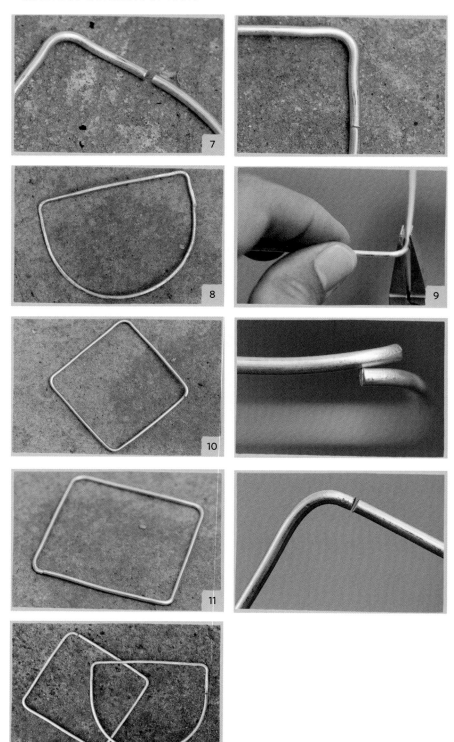

Half portion cuff

A stylish deviation from the standard ID bracelet, this piece can be made in brass, copper or sterling silver (if you are feeling posh-ish). Find a local engraver and have them add words on the face for all to see, or as a wee secret on the interior.

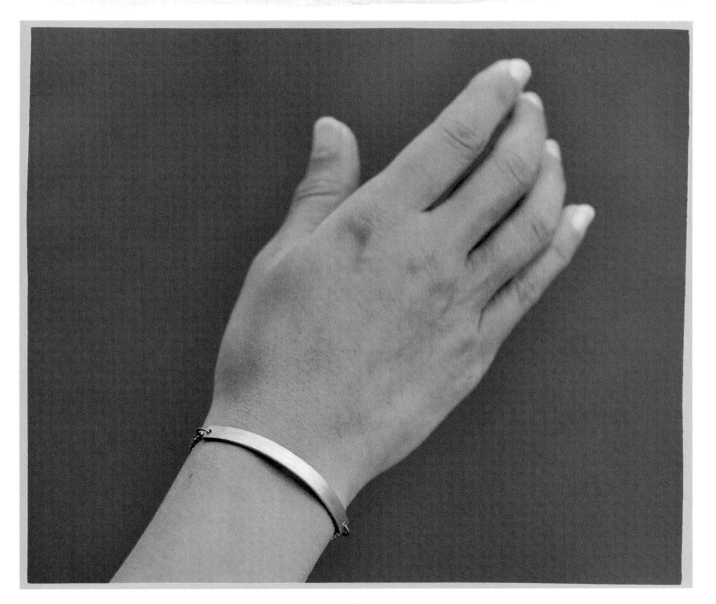

BITS YOU'LL NEED

• 2½" (6.4 cm) length of 0.064" x 0.25" copper strip (usually sold in 1' [30.5 cm] increments)
• 4"–5" (10.2–12.7 cm) length of copper curb chain
• One 9mm copper spring clasp
• Four 5mm copper jump rings, 16 gauge
• One 7mm copper jump ring, 16 gauge

TOOLS

• Drill
• #52 drill bit
• Safety glasses
• Jeweler's saw
• #6 saw blades
• V-board bench pin with clamp
• Chain-nose pliers
• Flat-nose pliers
• Nylon-jaw pliers
• Steel bench block
• File
• Sandpaper or sanding sponge

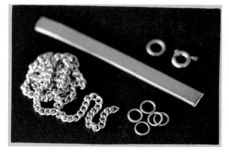

1. Measure and mark a 2½-inch (6.4 cm) length on the brass strip. Holding the strip firmly on a bench pin, cut to length with the saw.

2. Round the corners with a file.

3. Curve to fit by bending on a steel bench block, pressing with your fingers. Curve ends with nylon-jaw pliers if necessary.

4. Sand edges smooth, working from coarse- to fine-grit sandpaper. With a fine grit, texture the surface for a soft brushed look.

5. Drill a hole in either end, large enough to accommodate your jump ring.

6. Measure your wrist and determine how much chain you need to finish the bracelet to fit. Cut chain into two lengths.

7. With 5mm jump rings, attach the chain to one end of your curved piece, and attach the spring clasp to the chain end.

8. Attach the second length of chain to the opposite side of the curved piece with a 5mm jump ring, and attach the 7mm jump ring to the chain end with the last 5mm jump ring.

9. Think of something incredibly witty or sweet to get engraved on your piece, or simply wear as is.

Hammered Bangles

Soft facets and a golden sheen highlight an understated silhouette—perfect to wear on their own or work into a sea of arm ornaments.

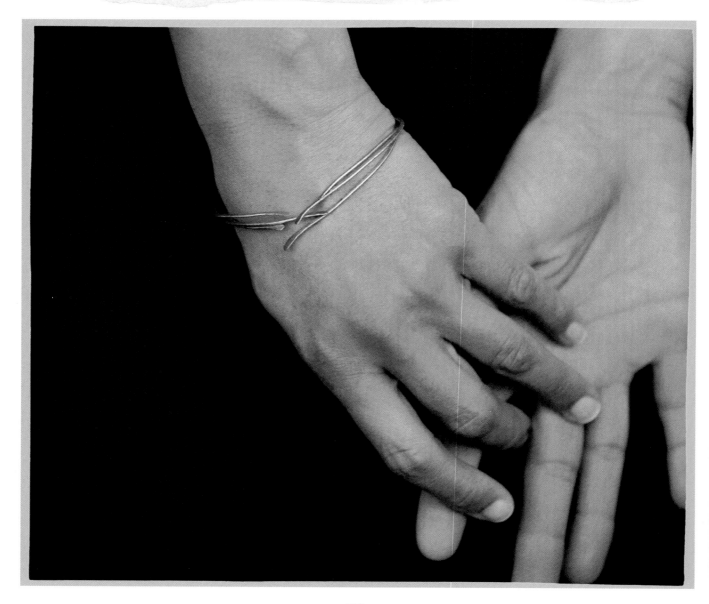

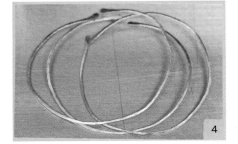

BITS YOU'LL NEED

• 16-gauge brass wire (you'll need 7"–8" [17.8–20.3 cm] per bangle)

TOOLS

• Metal shears or wire snips
• Hammer
• Steel bench block
• Suede sandbag (optional)
• File

1. Cut your wire to fit and shape into rounds. Starting at one end, hammer all the way around.

2. Hammer the ends until they are slightly spatulate.

3. Moving back to the center, begin hammering again, working from the center out until the bangle has a slight curve.

4. File any rough edges and make a few more.

hook and eye bracelet

Hammered brass and lush ribbon in a punchy neon velvet (or whatever color you please) join together to make a contrasting, oh-so-attractive twosome.

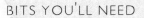

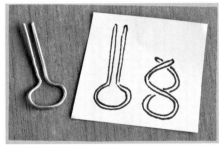

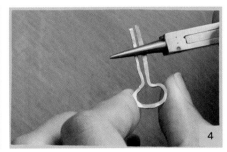

BITS YOU'LL NEED
- 4" (10.2 cm) length of 16-gauge brass wire
- 3½" (8.9 cm) length of 16-gauge brass wire
- 6½" (16.5 cm) length of ½" (1.3 cm) ribbon (elastic velvet is awesome, by the way)
- Thread
- Template (page 212)

TOOLS
- Round-nose pliers
- Flat-nose pliers
- Wire snips
- Hammer
- Steel bench block
- Suede sandbag (optional)
- File
- Needle

1. With the 4-inch (10.2 cm) length of wire, following the template, shape your hook piece with your fingers and round-nose pliers.

2. With the 3½-inch (8.9 cm) length of wire, following the template, shape your eye piece. The wire should overlap at the base by a few millimeters.

3. Hammer both pieces until flat. File any rough edges.

4. With a pair of round-nose pliers, bend the hook over.

5. Thread your ribbon through the base of the hook and stitch.

6. Thread the other end of the ribbon through the base of the eye, fit to size, trim and stitch. Easy peasy!

infinity bracelet

Make your own diminutive charm for this itty-bitty beautiful piece.

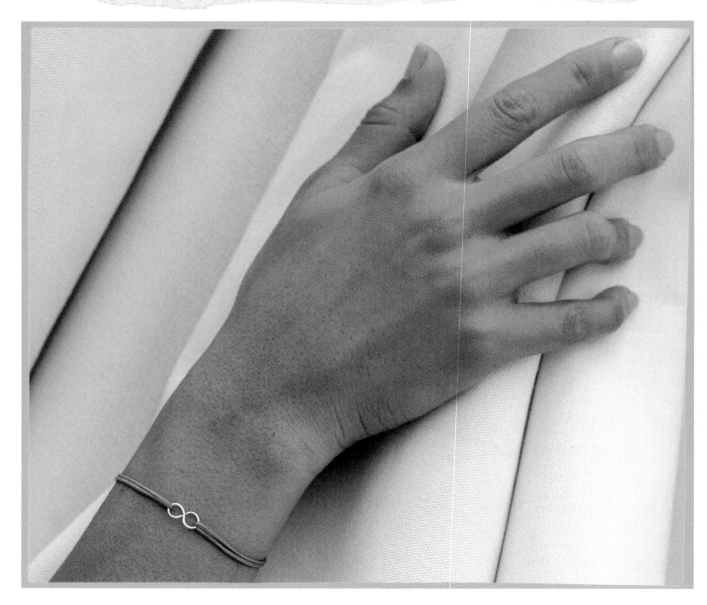

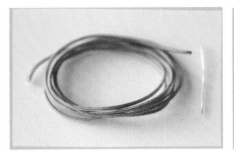

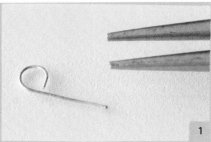

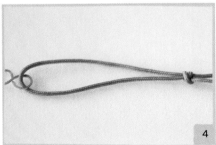

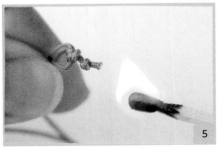

BITS YOU'LL NEED
• 18-gauge brass wire, 1" (2.5 cm) plus extra for mishaps
• 12" (30.5 cm) length of Chinese knotting cord

TOOLS
• Scissors
• Round-nose pliers
• Flat-nose pliers
• Wire snips
• Hammer
• Steel bench block
• Suede sandbag (optional)
• Lighter or matches

1. Cut a 1-inch (2.5 cm) length of wire. With a pair of round-nose pliers, shape into a figure eight.

2. Hammer. It doesn't take much with thin wire.

3. Thread cord through one side of your figure eight. Finish with a slip knot (see techniques, page 211).

4. Repeat on the opposite side.

5. Trim ends and melt with a match or lighter.

6. Rack your brain for more awesome shapes you can make to keep this sweet little thing in good company.

Nutty Bangle

Combining industrial elements with rustic detail, brass hardware adds unexpected movement and shine.

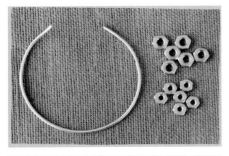

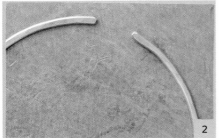

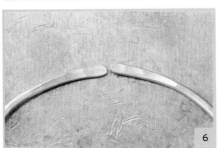

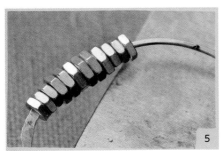

BITS YOU'LL NEED

- 12-gauge brass wire (you'll need 7"–8" [17.8–20.3 cm])
- Six #10-32 brass machine screw nuts
- Six #6-32 brass machine screw nuts

TOOLS

- Heavy-duty wire cutters
- Hammer
- Steel bench block
- Suede sandbag (optional)
- File

1. File the end of your wire so it is rounded and no sharp edges remain.

2. Hammer lightly all the way around. The nuts should slide on easily, so don't go too . . . nuts.

3. Center the hardware. You'll be hammering your piece about ⅜ inch (1 cm) away (marked) from the center grouping, on either side.

4. Begin hammering at the marked point. Hammer until the nuts can no longer slip over this joint, but take care not to overwork the metal or use the edge of the hammer, as you may cause the metal to snap. Hammer out from this area gradually, creating an even taper.

5. Slide the hardware over and repeat step 4 on the other side.

6. Hammer the ends until they are slightly spatulate.

7. Bolt this outfit-anchoring piece to your wrist stat.

washer bracelet

With a little texturing, brass washers from your local hardware shop gain a cool worn-in look that we love.

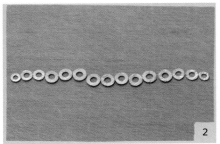

BITS YOU'LL NEED

- Two 6S brass washers
- Four 8S brass washers
- Nine 10S brass washers
- Fourteen 8x6mm jump rings, 18 gauge
- Two 9mm jump rings, 16 gauge
- One 6x7mm jump ring, 18 gauge
- One 15x9mm lobster clasp

TOOLS

- Hammer
- Steel bench block
- Suede sandbag (optional)
- Chain-nose pliers
- Flat-nose pliers

1. Hammer your washers, taking care not to hammer your fingers. Use the edge of the hammer face to get little indents and lines.

2. Arrange your pieces and link together with 8x6mm jump rings. We placed one each of the smallest on the very ends, followed by two of the medium-size washers, grouping the largest in the center.

3. When all washers are linked, attach two 19mm jump rings to one end, linking each to the other. On the opposite end, attach the clasp with a 6x7mm jump ring.

4. Hey, Home Depot, we did this.

copper bangle

One more to add to the raid-the-hardware list: the simple twisted look of this industrial-inspired bangle. Usually sold in 1-foot (30.5 cm) increments, this wire can be cut to length by the hardware store staff if you ask nicely. Just be sure to tape the ends so they don't unravel. This is a quick and inexpensive piece, perfect for making in batches for giftables.

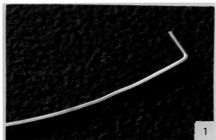

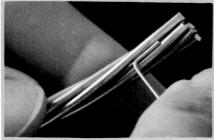

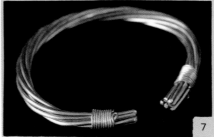

BITS YOU'LL NEED

- 7½" (19.1 cm) length of 6-stranded bare copper wire
- 20-gauge copper wire

TOOLS

- Flat-nose pliers
- Metal shears or wire snips
- Heavy-duty wire cutters
- File

1. Make a bend in your 20-gauge wire ⅜ inch (1 cm) from the end. Place into a furrow between two of the wire strands of the 6-stranded wire, ¾ inch (1.9 cm) from the end.

2. Begin wrapping as shown, keeping the wire as tight as possible. When you make enough rounds to cover the edge of the wire underneath, leave an additional ⅜ inch (1 cm), then trim your wire.

3. Tuck the end of the wire in underneath the wrapped wire, in the furrow between two of the wire strands in the 6-stranded wire. You can use a pair of pliers to wiggle it in as much as possible. It should be difficult to get it in particularly far.

4. Twist the excess with a pair of pliers and flatten against the piece.

5. Repeat steps 1–4 on the opposite end.

6. File the ends of your wire until smooth to the touch.

7. Working from end to end with your fingers, gently curve to fit.

plastic

superfantastic plastic is hard to beat for its durability and range of finishes. it can mimic natural forms that aren't otherwise easily converted into wearable objects, such as precious materials (ivory, we're talking to you), or just exist as something all its own. better still, we're blessed with so many products and tools that are easily accessible and fantastic to work with in regular old life—no lab or mega factory required.

ivory bracelet

Cruelty-free, Masecraft's faux ivory sheet has subtle striations that are absolutely to die for. It cuts, files and sands beautifully.

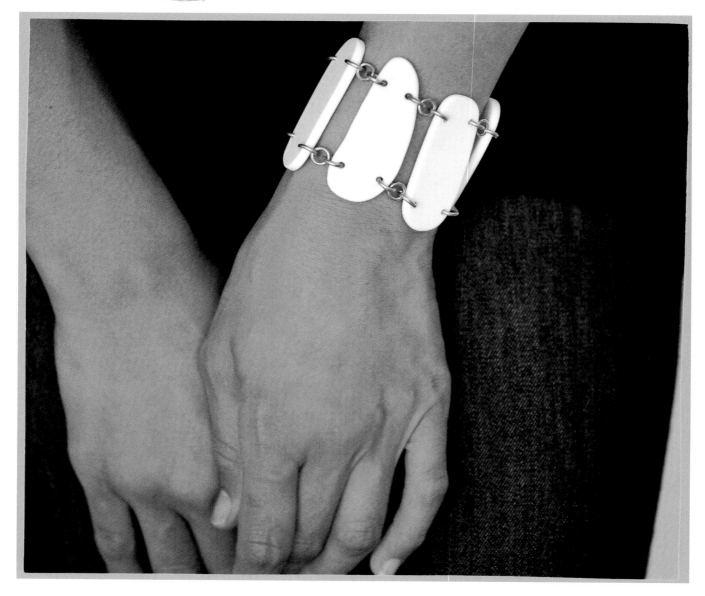

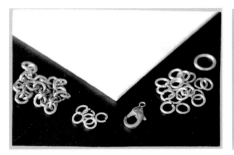

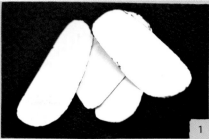

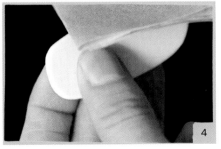

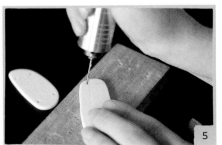

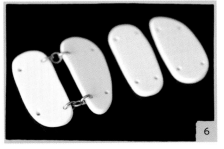

BITS YOU'LL NEED

- 4" x 5" (10.2 x 12.7 cm) sheet of alternative ivory, ⅜" (1 cm) thick
- 3"–7" (7.6–17.8 cm) length of chain
- One 10mm jump ring, 14–16 gauge
- Twenty-four 8mm jump rings, 14–16 gauge
- One lobster clasp (ours is 20 mm long)
- Template (page 212)

TOOLS

- Fine-point permanent marker
- Jeweler's saw
- V-board bench pin with clamp
- #2 saw blades
- Sandpaper or sanding sponges
- File
- Drill
- #30 drill bit
- Safety glasses
- Chain-nose pliers
- Flat-nose pliers
- Craft knife

1. Make a copy of the template and cut out shapes with a craft knife. Trace shapes onto your alternative ivory sheet with a marker. Keep pieces close to edge and close together to conserve material.

2. Beginning at the edge, start cutting your pieces out one by one.

3. Shape with a file.

4. Working from a coarse- to fine-grit sandpaper, sand until edges are rounded and smooth.

5. Drill holes.

6. Arrange and link together with jump rings, keeping links parallel.

7. When all pieces are linked, try it on and figure out how much chain you'll need to fit. Depending on your wrist size, you may need very little. Our bracelet has two lengths of chain on each side that meet to form a triangle.

8. Connect chains to pieces, and to each other. Connect lobster clasp to one end with a jump ring.

9. Add a 10mm jump ring to the other end.

10. One hundred percent cruelty-free, sawing and filing aside.

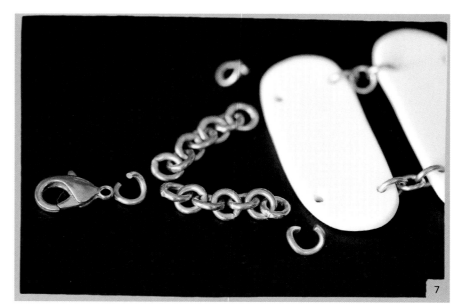

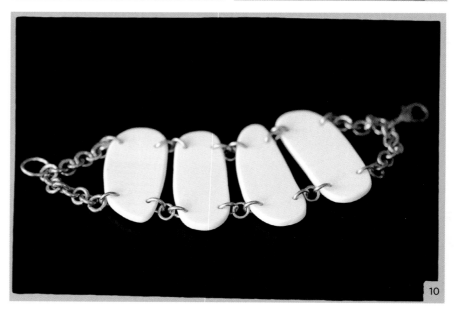

marbled Bracelet

Mimicking classically cool and gorgeous marble, this bracelet is sure to surprise and delight. All those modeling clay squishing skills you acquired as a child are finally put to good use.

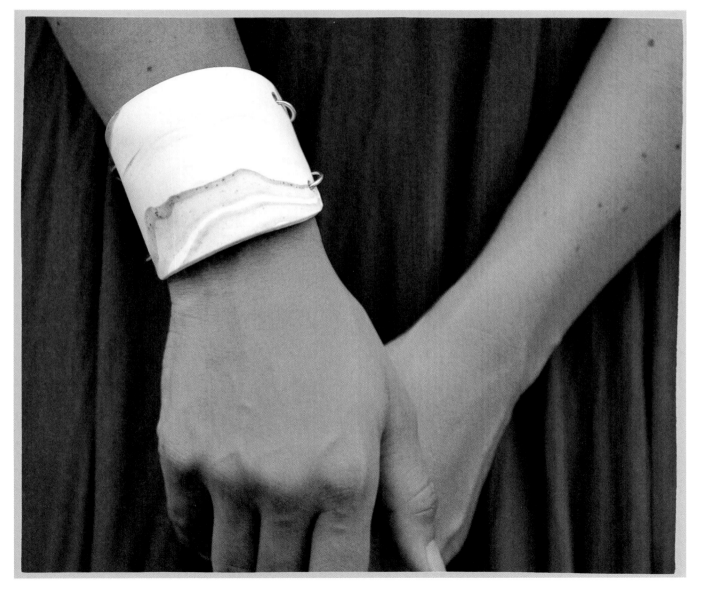

BITS YOU'LL NEED

• 2 oz (57 g) blocks of Fimo polymer clay: Light Gray, Granite, White
• 5"–8" (12.7–20.3 cm) length of chunky unsoldered chain (you should see a seam on each link)
• Five 10–12mm jump rings, 14–18 gauge
• Three 8mm jump rings, 16–18 gauge
• One lobster clasp (ours is 20 mm long)
• Template (page 212)

TOOLS

• Ovenproof glass or mug (roughly the circumference of your arm)
• Craft knife
• Acrylic polymer clay roller
• Drinking straw
• Smooth silicone baking mat (optional)
• Chain-nose pliers
• Flat-nose pliers

1. Make a copy of the template and cut out. Preheat your oven to 275°F (135°C).

2. Cut off pieces of clay and roll out into snakes the length of the template, working until soft and pliable. You'll need a thin line of Light Gray, a thin line of Granite and lots of White (about one part each of Light Gray and Granite to six parts White). You can lay them out to approximate coverage. You want your final slab to be about ⅜ inch (1 cm) thick.

3. Stack the lines and press into each other. Fold in half.

4. Continue folding until blended, three or four more times, then roll into a short tube.

5. On a smooth surface (a smooth silicone baking mat is GREAT), roll out to ⅜ inch (1 cm) thick with the acrylic roller. It should overlap your template a bit. If not, nudge the shape a bit and roll to suit. Make sure there are no cracks.

6. Lay the template on top, and with a craft knife carefully cut out your piece. If you've got scraps, consider making a pair of earrings.

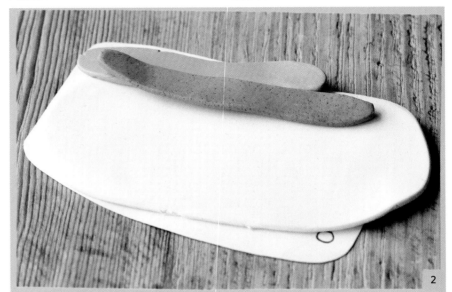

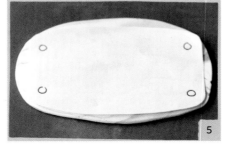

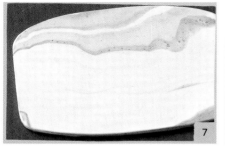

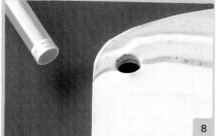

7. Smooth the edges with your finger until slightly beveled, taking care not to push the piece out of shape.

8. With a straw, punch four holes in the corners—but not too close to the edge! Twist and pull up, and the middle bits should hopefully come with the straw.

9. Drape your piece over the glass or other ovenproof form you are using. Gently push the edges down to curve and stick to the glass without indenting. Smooth any fingerprints.

10. Bake according to manufacturer's instructions. Let cool completely before attempting to remove unless you really want to do it all over! Patience is a virtue.

11. Lay out your piece and configure your chain length. Separate chain into desired lengths by twisting open with chain-nose and flat-nose pliers.

12. Attach all your lengths with jump rings. Connect the lengths on one side to a lobster clasp with an 8mm jump ring, forming a triangle, and do the same on the opposite side, connecting to another 8mm ring and finally a 10–12mm ring.

13. Wilma Flintstone, don't be jealous.

starfish cuff

If you've ever draped a starfish on your palm as a child, this will bring back some warm fuzzy memories (or have you totally creeped out after you've seen videos of them eating dead things). You can easily find starfish in most craft shops. Choose one that fits almost all the way around your arm, with enough room to slip on and off.

BITS YOU'LL NEED

- Starfish (about 5" [12.7 cm] across)
- ½ lb (225 g) silicone mold putty
- Premo! Sculpey or similar polymer clay (enough to fill in volume of starfish)
- Gold spray paint
- Clear acrylic sealer

TOOLS

- Tapered ovenproof glass or mug (roughly the circumference of your arm)
- Craft knife

1. With your starfish at the ready, mix the putty according to the manufacturer's instructions. You've usually got 2 to 3 minutes until it sets, so work quickly! The color should be evenly mixed.

2. Once mixed, shape the putty into a rough starfish form.

3. Place your starfish on top (with the face you'd like to mold pressing into the putty) and start lifting and forming the putty around it.

4. The putty should go a few millimeters up past the side, forming a little wall, but leaving the rear face of the starfish unobstructed.

5. Following the manufacturer's instructions allow mold to set. Remove the starfish.

6–7

11

6. Preheat your oven according to manufacturer's instructions. Cut off a slab of clay, then knead with your fingers until it is soft and malleable. Roll out to form a rough double arm for your starfish and press into mold.

7. Continuing until mold is full, begin pressing and working clay into mold. Ensure there are no air pockets, cracks or seams and that all the clay is smooth, even and bonded to itself. Imperfections could weaken your bracelet and cause potential breakage.

8. Flip mold over and carefully peel it back, working one arm at a time, then easing out the center.

9. If you have any cracks, breaks or imperfections, replace the clay into the mold and work it some more. The more you work it, the stronger it will be. Once you are satisfied, trim the edges with a sharp knife and smooth rough edges with your fingers.

10. Figure out your fit by draping the starfish across your arm. The longest part should curve around the smallest part of your arm for best staying power.

11. Fit the starfish over your glass, mimicking the taper of your arm. Press the arms onto the glass so they aren't just flopping straight down.

12. Bake according to manufacturer's instructions (about 15 minutes). Let cool completely before attempting to remove unless you really want to do it all over! Patience is a virtue.

13. Once cool, remove. Following the manufacturer's instructions, spray a coat of gold inside and out, allowing drying time in between coats and sides. Finish with a clear coat. Let dry overnight or until paint is fully cured.

14. Secretly relive all your little mermaid fantasies.

13

14

gold rush bangle

Suspended flakes of flashing gold wink and shimmer in the most captivating way. You can leave your resin crystal clear or play with your own color tints. Make multiple sizes and stack together for a shimmering statement.

BITS YOU'LL NEED

• Loose gold leaf flakes or gold leaf sheet (you might have some left over from the Doily Cuff on page 94)
• EasyCast clear casting epoxy
• Transparent resin dye: blue, red, yellow
• Mold release spray (optional)
• Clear gloss resin spray sealer

TOOLS

• Plastic bangle mold with 2⅜" (6 cm) internal diameter, ¼" (6 mm) height, ⅜" (1 cm) width (you might need a larger or smaller size)
• Disposable plastic measuring cup (you can clean with acetone and reuse)
• Popsicle stick
• Pipette (optional)
• File
• Waterproof sandpaper or sanding sponges (120, 600 and 1200 grit)

1. Spray mold with mold release and allow to dry completely; this makes it a bit easier to get your piece out. Working in a well-ventilated area, follow the manufacturer's instructions and mix your resin. You'll need 3 ounces (84 g) to fill the mold we used. Fold smoothly to minimize bubbles in the mix. We mixed ours more vigorously for a little more texture.

2. Add color and blend. To get our gray-purple, we used two drops of blue, two drops of red and one drop of yellow. You can use a pipette if your dye does not have a dropper. Blend.

3. Add gold flakes. If you are using sheet, you'll want to scrape them off carefully 1 or 2 inches (2.5 to 5.1 cm) at a time so they don't clump.

4. Blend.

5. Pour into mold in a smooth stream (smaller and smoother for fewer bubbles). Take care not to overfill or you'll be sanding and filing all the extra flashing. If any large pieces of gold are coming up at the surface, push down with a pin. Pop any surface bubbles. Cover with a bowl or container to keep dust out.

6. When your resin is cured (follow the manufacturer's instructions on drying time), pop the bangle out of the mold. Twist and push from the back. Be patient and don't worry about breaking your mold, because you will feel like you are about to. They are sturdy and will regain their original shape with a little help.

7. If necessary, file your edges smooth.

8. Working in a bowl of water or sink with wet sandpaper or sanding sponges, sand from a fine to extra-fine grain, smoothing any imperfections.

9. Your bracelet will look a bit scuffed—don't worry. Time for the gloss spray! Follow the manufacturer's instructions for number of coats and drying time.

10. Superfancy and superaddictive.

swirl bangle

Swirls of color embody a blend of breezy California chic and up-to-the-minute feel in a bold, modern shape. We used a silicone mold we purchased on Etsy, but you can always reuse the mold for the Gold Rush Bangle on page 183 along with the same proportions of epoxy.

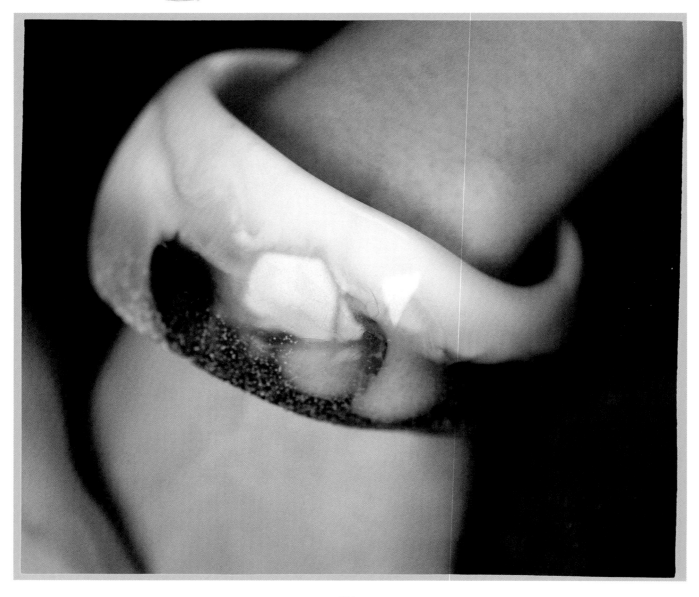

BITS YOU'LL NEED
- EasyCast clear casting epoxy
- Transparent resin dye: blue, yellow
- Opaque resin dye: white
- Mold release spray (optional)
- Clear gloss resin spray sealer (optional)

TOOLS
- Plastic or silicone bangle mold
- Two disposable plastic measuring cups (you can clean with acetone and reuse)
- Two Popsicle sticks
- File
- Waterproof sandpaper or sanding sponges (120, 600 and 1200 grit)

1. Spray mold with mold release and allow to dry completely; this makes it a bit easier to get your piece out. Following the manufacturer's instructions, mix a batch of resin in the plastic cup. Fold smoothly to minimize bubbles in the mix.

2. Pour one-third of the resin into the second cup, then add blue and yellow (or whatever colors you please) until desired hue is achieved. Mix a few drops of opaque white in until you are happy. If you need to add more color, go ahead.

3. Add opaque white dye a few drops at a time to the remaining two-thirds of the resin and blend until you are content with the look.

4. Holding a cup in each hand, begin pouring the white resin first in a small, smooth stream. When it gets past half of the mold, begin pouring the colored resin. Continue pouring both in even streams. Take care not to overfill. Pop any surface bubbles. Cover with a bowl or container to keep out dust and particles.

5. When your resin is cured (follow the manufacturer's instructions on drying time), pop the bangle out of the mold. Twist and push from the back. Be patient and don't worry about breaking your mold, because you will feel like you are about to. They are sturdy and will regain their original shape with a little help.

6. If necessary, file your edges smooth.

7. Working over a bowl of water or sink with wet sandpaper or sanding sponges, sand from a fine to extra-fine grain, smoothing any imperfections.

8. You can sand the entire surface of your bracelet for a matte look, or if you'd prefer a gloss finish, coat with gloss spray. Follow the manufacturer's instructions for number of coats and drying time.

pleather knot bracelet

I wasn't a huge fan of the plastic strips when they first arrived in the mail, but once heated they took on a great leathery look from handling and I was officially won over. These are so small and sweet and zippy-fast to make, there's no excuse not to make them in stacks of multiple hues.

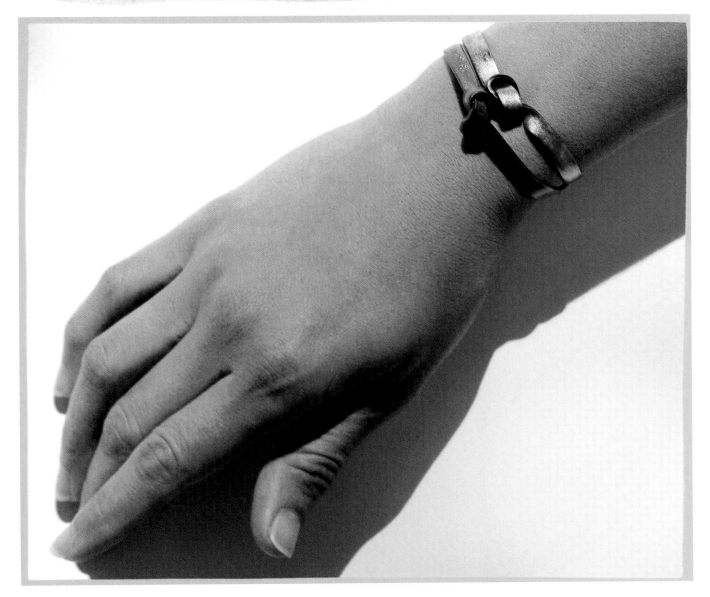

BITS YOU'LL NEED

- 7" (17.8 cm) length of Friendly plastic strip
- One 9x6mm lobster clasp
- Two 5mm jump rings, 18–20 gauge
- 1"–2" (2.5–5.1 cm) length of chain (something easy for your clasp to catch onto)

TOOLS

- Drill
- #55 drill bit
- Safety glasses
- Skillet or low-sided pot
- Bowl of ice water
- Bottle with a circumference that's slightly smaller than your wrist
- Cooking thermometer
- Scissors
- Chain-nose pliers
- Flat-nose pliers

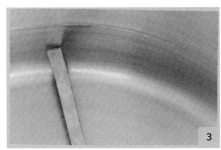

1. Fill a skillet with 1 inch (2.5 cm) of water. Heat to 150°F (65°C). Disclosure: I let the water get too hot the first try and ended up with a melted mess.

2. Cut a strip of plastic 7 inches (17.8 cm) long and ¼ inch (6 mm) wide.

3. Submerge in the hot water for about 30 seconds until it becomes a bit wavy. Do not submerge it for too long (maximum 60 seconds) or you'll ruin the finish.

4. Working quickly, remove from the water and knot in the center. Place over a bottle, holding the sides down so they taper, and wait for a few moments before plunging your piece into cold water.

5. After a few seconds, take out, dry and drill a hole on each end.

6. Connect your chain to one end with a jump ring and the lobster clasp to the other with a jump ring.

7. Repeat, repeat, repeat for a stack of greatness.

Naiad Bracelet

If you didn't play with Shrinky Dinks as a child, I'm giving you good reason to now. Follow the templates or find something else awesome to trace and color in. I prefer drilling the pieces after they've been shrunk, but you can punch the holes out with a paper punch before baking.

BITS YOU'LL NEED

• Two 8" x 10" (20.3 x 25.4 cm) clear Shrinky Dink sheets
• One 9x6mm lobster clasp
• Twenty-six 5mm jump rings, 18–20 gauge
• 1" (2.5 cm) length of chain (something easy for your clasp to catch onto)
• Brown paper
• Template (page 212)

TOOLS

• Fine-point permanent black marker
• Colored pencils
• Scissors
• Chain-nose pliers
• Flat-nose pliers
• ⅛" (3 mm) paper punch (or drill and #55 drill bit)

1. With a permanent marker, place the sheet over the template and trace outline.

2. Cut out, leaving a ¼-inch (6 mm) border. If not drilling after baking, punch holes where marked.

3. Color.

4. Heat oven to 325°F (160°C). Line a baking sheet with brown paper, folding edges up so you can grab it easily.

5. Place colored cutouts on paper, colored side up, making sure they have a little room and nothing is touching.

6. Place sheet into heated oven. Watch those pieces like a hawk (they should take 1 to 3 minutes). Look for them to curl up and flatten again. Once they are flat, pull them out! If any pieces have curled onto themselves, gently pull apart and flatten. Reheat if you need to.

7. Connect your pieces with three 5mm jump rings, keeping links parallel.

8. When all pieces are connected, attach your chain to one end with a jump ring and the lobster clasp to the other with a jump ring.

9. Good clean fun accomplished.

wood

weathered or polished, delicate or chunky, wood is always in season. while i loved the hours i spent in the woodworking studio at design school, i won't torture you with table saws, planers or steam bending. nuh-uh. only easy and entertaining bits that will make you feel just the right amount of handy.

lace Bangles

Craft shops such as Michaels stock a great selection of inexpensive wood cutouts, including the great lacy wood "doilies" we use in this project. With little effort you can transform them into sweet, femme and witty wearables.

1

2

3

4

5

6

BITS YOU'LL NEED
- One bangle that fits you well
- 4" (10.2 cm) laser-cut wood "doilies"
- 100-grit sandpaper
- White acrylic paint

TOOLS
- Sponge brush
- Drill (most bit sizes will do once saw blade can fit through hole)
- Safety glasses
- Adjustable 4" (10.2 cm) jeweler's saw
- #2 saw blades
- V-board bench pin with clamp

1. Center your bangle on a doily. With a pencil, trace the inside circumference.

2. If a cut or hole in the doily overlaps with your pencil line, you can skip to step 3. If not, you'll need to drill a small hole along the line. Be sure to wear your safety glasses.

3. Insert your saw blade through the hole, back into the frame and secure. See techniques (page 209) for detailed instructions on using a jeweler's saw.

4. Working on the V-board bench pin, saw along your pencil line. Use smooth strokes and gently rotate the piece as your blade moves forward. Continue cutting the centers of all your pieces out in the same manner.

5. When all the centers are cut out, you are ready to sand. Sand gently to smooth out the edge so it wears comfortably.

6. Finish with a coat or two of paint, dabbing each coat on lightly and evenly with a sponge brush. Allow the pieces to dry between coats.

pastille Bracelet

Playful and fresh, wood dowel plugs from your local hardware store line up for a contemporary hit in punchy hues.

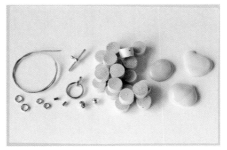

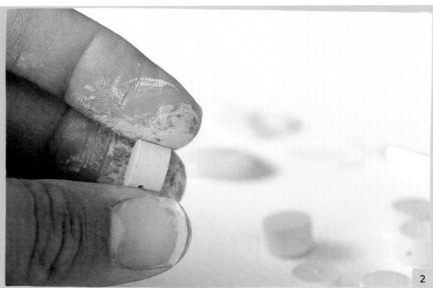

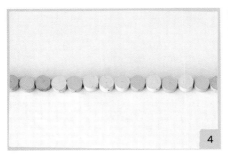

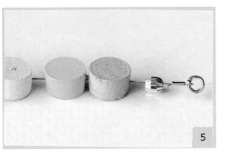

BITS YOU'LL NEED

• Eighteen (possibly more) ⅜" (1 cm) flat head wood dowel plugs
• Three colors of acrylic paint (your choice)
• One 12mm round toggle clasp
• Two 5.5mm jump rings, 18–20 gauge
• Two 4.5mm jump rings, 18–20 gauge
• Two 3x2mm crimp tubes
• Two 3–5mm round brass beads (hole must be larger than 2 mm in diameter to fit over crimp tubes)
• 9" (22.9 cm) length of beading wire, 0.024" diameter

TOOLS

• Drill
• #55 drill bit
• Safety glasses
• Paintbrush
• Crimping pliers
• Wire snips
• Nylon-jaw pliers
• Chain-nose pliers
• Flat-nose pliers

1. Get your supercool safety glasses on. Carefully drill through the side of your plugs.

2. Determine how many of each color bead you'd like and separate into batches. Paint your first set of plugs with a thin coat of acrylic. Two coats should be sufficient, but you can go for a third for extra vibrancy. Give the pieces a few minutes to dry in between coats as well as after the final coat.

3. Paint the second and third sets while the previous set is drying.

4. Once all of your plugs have been painted and are dry, lay them out in stringing order.

5. Thread and crimp your beading wire onto a securely closed 4.5mm jump ring. See techniques (page 209) for detailed instructions on crimping. Thread your first brass bead over the closed crimp tube and string the painted beads (maiden name: plugs) in your desired order.

6. When you've finished stringing your beads, add another brass bead to finish, then slip on your crimp tube, and loop through a 4.5mm jump ring.

7. Since the beads are slightly tapered, you won't need much extra room for them to flex. Get the crimp tube as snug to the last bead as possible and crimp the tube closed.

8. Attach the toggle bar to one end with two 5.5mm jump rings and the ring directly to the other end.

9. Who said arm candy?

watercolor bangles

Rich color palettes and easy shapes collide to create a striking set of bangles that promise to add a modern yet down-to-earth feel to your look.

BITS YOU'LL NEED

- Unfinished natural wood bangles (a light-colored wood works best)
- Acrylic paint (we used blue, green and a spot of purple)
- Water

TOOLS

- Paintbrush
- Shallow dish
- Paper towels

1. Blend your paint colors to your desired hue, add a splash of water and mix until you've got a fairly liquid consistency. You can continue to mix in different colors bit by bit for each new bangle to create complementary shades and hues.

2. Paint your first bangle. Brush and blot your paint on. No need to be perfectly even.

3. Let the coat sit for about 30 seconds, then wipe or blot off excess.

4. Your piece should dry quickly. If you'd like a little more variation in the finish, continue adding layers of color, letting each coat soak in for another 30–60 seconds before blotting again. Repeat until you're satisfied.

5. Switching up your color, paint another.

6. And maybe another. And another? Okay, one more.

beach treasure bracelet

For a few dollars you can find driftwood pieces by Panacea at Jo-Ann, bagged and ready to go. If you are feeling truly handy, blessed with time and live near a beach, you can create your own lengths with the help of a small saw and loads of sanding. Either way you'll end up with a brilliantly bohemian bauble.

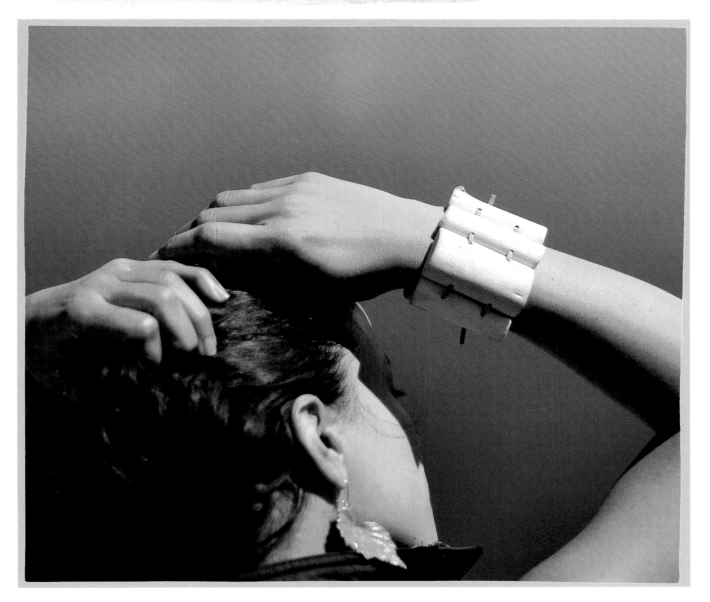

BITS YOU'LL NEED

• Enough 2½" (6.4 cm)-long pieces of driftwood to span 6"–7" (15.2–17.8 cm) when stacked side by side
• 32" (81.3 cm) length of natural-colored suede (or faux suede) lace
• 100-grit sandpaper
• 6" (15.2 cm) length of 26-gauge wire

TOOLS

• Pencil
• Drill
• #30 drill bit
• Safety glasses
• Scissors
• Wire snips
• Sandpaper
• Needle or hole punch
• Ruler

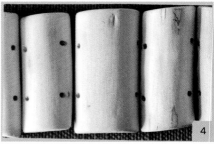

1. Select the best pieces for your desired length. Mark the drill points on your first piece. Ours are ¾ inch (1.9 cm) in from the outside edge and just under ¼ inch (6 mm) from the base.

2. Line up all of your pieces. Using a ruler, continue marking the drill points on all.

3. Get your supercool safety glasses on. Carefully drill through your pieces. Lightly sand rough areas if necessary.

4. Line your pieces up in stringing order.

5. With a needle or leather punch, put a small hole in one end of your lace and thread a 6-inch (15.2 cm) length of wire through. Double over the top end and twist to secure.

6. Leading with the wire "needle" you've just made, thread the lace through the top set of holes on all of your pieces.

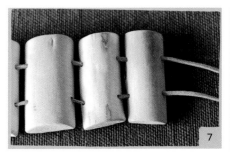

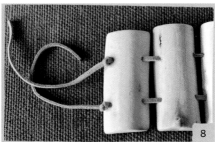

7. Double back through the bottom set of holes.

8. Pull the lace so it is even on both sides, leaving a little gap in between the wood pieces so they can bend easily. Snip the doubled-over bit to make two separate strands and make an overhand knot in each strand against the last slat of wood. Repeat on the other end.

9. Tie it on.

tools + materials

TOOLS

Acrylic clay roller—rolls smooth, even sheets of polymer clay.

Aviation shears, heavy-duty wire cutters or sprue cutters—used for heavier gauge wire.

Bead boards—allow you to lay out bead designs without having things roll all over the place. Measurements are marked, but you should always measure again with a ruler or tape (and try on) before finishing your piece.

Bench pin—used to support work while sawing, filing and more; they are available in several styles. For the projects in this book, a V-slot bench pin with a clamp is your best bet, and you can easily secure it to (and remove it from) a table.

Binder clips—great for securing cord ends to keep beads from escaping; line the insides with two layers of painter's tape for a great grip.

Chain-nose pliers—the ultimate does-a-bit-of-everything plier; used to open and close loops and jump rings, close end findings and pull cord. You can wrap these (and flat-nose pliers) with a bit of painter's tape as a substitute for nylon-jaw pliers, particularly handy when you need a more precise tool.

Craft knife—handy for trimming clay, leather and other materials as well as cutting out templates.

Crimping pliers—used to compress crimp tubes onto themselves. Available in multiple sizes; we use a regular size for the relevant projects in this book.

Dremel—drill, grind, sand, polish and cut with this handy rotary tool. Note that you'll be using smaller-than-usual metal twist drill bits for many of the projects, so you'll need to buy the appropriate collets to fit them in addition to the ones that are usually supplied with the basic kit.

Drill bits—for metal projects, use high-speed metal twist drill bits with your Dremel (or other high-speed drill). You can find the smaller sizes through jewelry tool suppliers. Use a bit slightly larger than the gauge of your jump rings so they can move easily. You can use either wood or metal drill bits for plastic and resin.

Flat-nose pliers—great for materials that are thicker or need a sturdier grip; I often use these in conjunction with chain-nose pliers to open and close jump rings and chain.

Foil—used to catch hot glue drips and protect surfaces.

Hammer—you can purchase a ball-peen jewelry hammer, or if you already have one around, just use a regular household hammer, which works perfectly for all of the projects in this book.

Jeweler's automatic center punch—this spring-loaded punch will mark metal with a simple push. Use to make a starting point for your drill bit so it doesn't wander.

Jeweler's metal shears—these come with straight or curved blades and are used for cutting sheet metal. The curved blade is better for—you guessed it—cutting curves. Most shears work on sheet metals up to 20 gauge. They're also useful for snipping thinner chains and wires.

Loop-closing pliers—used to firmly close jump rings, but not an absolute necessity in your kit. I prefer working with chain-nose and flat-nose pliers instead.

Metal bench block—hardened steel surface to support your work while hammering, bending, flattening and stamping. Best used with a suede sandbag underneath.

Nylon-jaw pliers—similar to flat-nose pliers; used to close findings to prevent damaging the metal finish.

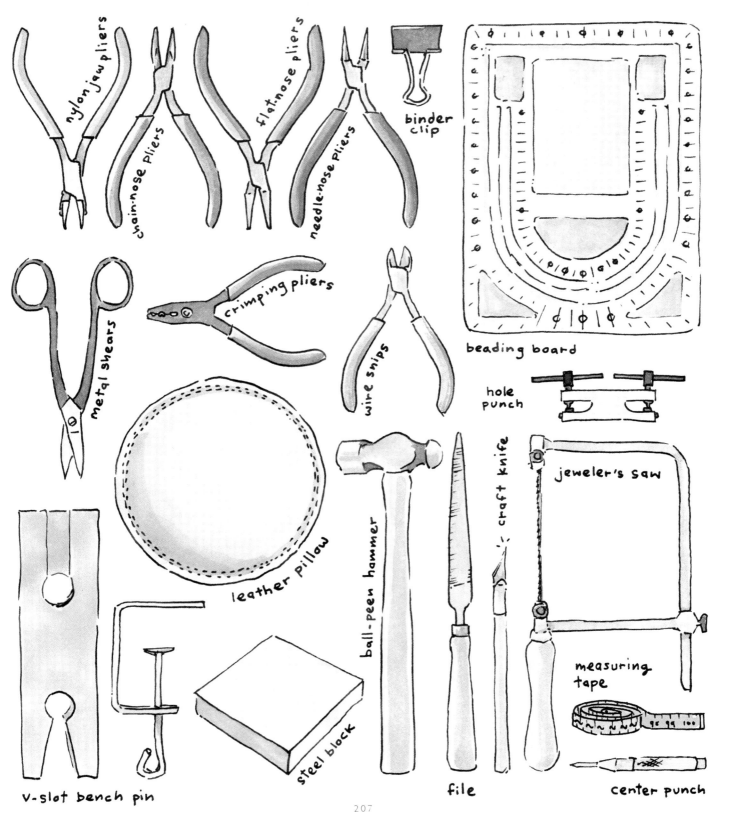

nylon jaw pliers

chain-nose pliers

flat-nose pliers

needle-nose pliers

binder clip

beading board

metal shears

crimping pliers

wire snips

hole punch

leather pillow

ball-peen hammer

file

craft knife

jeweler's saw

measuring tape

v-slot bench pin

steel block

center punch

Round-nose pliers—used to create loops and round bends. Use varying points of the tapered jaws to create different loop sizes or wider bends.

Rulers and measuring tape—measure, measure, measure your components and pieces in progress. Measuring tape is handy for getting wrist sizes right.

Safety glasses—inexpensive and easily procured at your local hardware shop. Wear them.

Sanding sponges and sponge pads—great for cleaning up and smoothing out pieces. Keep a selection of grits on hand. Work from heavier (to remove coarser burrs and shape) to fine (to smooth edges and add a brushed look).

Scissors—you might be familiar with these. Use to cut ribbon, cord, cloth and flexible plastic sheets.

Steel hole punch—twist to punch holes in leather and metals up to 3 millimeters thick.

Suede sandbag—placed under your bench block, this is used to dampen the vibration from hammering and protect your tabletop.

Wire cutters/wire snips—a great all-purpose cutter.

FINDINGS

Chain—connected links. You can find soldered and unsoldered chain. Soldered chain will need to be cut, while you can separate unsoldered chain with pliers.

Clasps—lobster, spring, toggle, button, hook and eye, and S-clasps are a few closure options. Choose styles and sizes that best suit your project.

Cord ends—glue cords in to finish.

Crimps—used with crimping pliers to secure beading wire.

Jump rings—gauged round or oval wire rings used to connect elements. They are available soldered and unsoldered in a range of metals, sizes and finishes.

Ribbon ends—flatten and clamp to finish ribbon bracelets.

CORDS + WIRES

Beading wire—flexible coated wire available in varying sizes. Use thinner sizes for smaller and lighter beads and thicker for heavier projects. No beading needles necessary!

Elastic—our projects use thicker elastic cords, which can be beaded without a needle and easily knotted off.

Metal wire—available in different metals and finishes. Lower number gauges are thicker, and get thinner as the gauge number increases.

Suede and leather lace—available in faux/vegan versions, it has a supple drape and loads of colors to choose from.

OTHER MATERIALS

Adhesives—E6000 works well for securing stretchy cord knots and adhering rhinestones. Pasco Fix does the same but instantly. Dab G-S Hypo Fabric Cement on tassel knots.

Beeswax—available at craft and health food shops; keep a block handy to lubricate your drill bits (simply drill into the beeswax block in between metal pieces).

Fabric stiffener—used to stiffen fabrics. Apply before shaping, then cured.

Fray Check—used on ribbon ends to prevent raveling.

Painter's tape—used to wrap tools to prevent marring surfaces, and to add padding to binder clips for clamping cords. Will not leave a sticky residue.

techniques

DRILLING

A Dremel is a great small tool for much more than drilling, and it can accommodate smaller twist drill bits with the right collet. Be sure to buy the correct drill bits for your project (metal, wood, plastic, etc.) and always wear safety glasses! Protect those peepers.

DRILLING TIPS

• Use a scrap wood block as a drill base—you don't want to damage a nice tabletop or your bit.

• Use a lubricant (beeswax works beautifully).

• Hold on to your piece because the drill can snag it and spin it dangerously.

• Start with a slower speed.

• Do not change your angle or wiggle the bit.

SAWING AND PIERCING

To insert the blade: Making sure the teeth are pointing down, clamp one end in place and finger-tighten the screw. Adjust the length of the saw so the tip of the blade overlaps the second grip by a few millimeters. Leaning the frame against your table, apply enough pressure to shorten the frame. Insert the loose blade end and tighten—when you stop compressing the frame it will spring back and place that tension on the blade.

Sawing should be done in a smooth rhythmic motion, lifting slightly on the return because the cut is made with the downstroke. Use a wooden bench pin to support your piece. Beeswax can help lubricate and make cutting smoother; periodically run a piece over the blade.

FILING

Because files cut on the downstroke, you should always lift and leave a bit of room on the return stroke to prevent the file's teeth from being pushed down, which will shorten its effectiveness and life.

STRETCHING CORD

Always cut your cord 3 to 4 inches (7.6–10.2 cm) longer than the length you need. Stretch your cord prior to use to prevent it from stretching out later on. Knot four to six times and finish with a tiny drop of E6000 adhesive to secure.

CRIMPING

Crimp pliers have two crimp-forming areas. One is lip shaped, for making the first crimp, and the second is used to round and close the crimp onto itself. First, place the crimp in the lip-shaped area, turning the wires so they align with the two indents on top. Squeeze to form a U shape. Then, rotate the crimp 90 degrees and crimp with the round area. Trim off any excess wire, or tuck into a bead and you are done! For photos of the process, see Gilded Waves Bracelet, page 10.

CRIMP COVERS

Crimp covers are a great way to add a polished finish to your piece. Simply slip over a crimped tube and squeeze together with the round area of your crimping pliers or nylon-jaw pliers. I prefer the latter because sometimes the crimp pliers can mar the finish if you're not terribly careful.

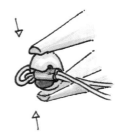

JUMP RINGS

One of the most essential little bits of many a project, jump rings must be closed securely. You can use a jump ring tool or loop-closing pliers, but I'm a big advocate for two pairs of pliers—flat-nosed and chain-nosed. Once you get used to them, it is just as speedy and you've got one less tool to buy and fish around for. To open a jump ring, pick up a jump ring near the seam with a pair of pliers and hold firmly. With a second pair of pliers, grab the other side near the seam and gently twist to open. To close, grasp each side of the jump ring near the seam and twist together. A wee bit of back-and-forth wiggle helps to get the ends flush and work hardens the metal, strengthening it.

WRAPPED LOOP LINK

With a pair of round-nose pliers, grip the wire about 1½ inches (3.8 cm) from the end. Bend to a 90-degree angle. Grip the wire in the angle and, with a pair of chain-nose pliers, grab the end and roll it around the barrel of the round-nose pliers to form a loop. Continue wrapping around the stem for one turn, just under the loop. Hold the loop in the chain-nose pliers and, with a pair of flat-nosed pliers, tightly wrap around two or three more turns. Trim any excess and squeeze the cut end flush with chain-nose pliers.

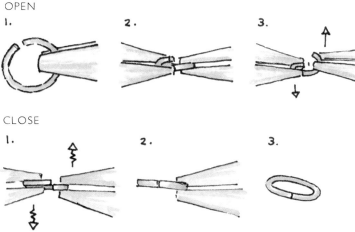

OPEN

CLOSE

SIMPLE LOOP

With a pair of round-nose pliers, grip the wire about ⅜ inch (1 cm) from the end. Bend to a 90-degree angle. Grip the very end of the wire, keeping the end in the center of the pliers where the barrels meet. Simply turn the pliers while applying pressure on the straight length just underneath the bend to form a loop. You may need to adjust the loop a bit so it is centered.

WRAPPED LOOP DANGLE

This is usually done to add a loop to a head pin after a bead has been strung onto it. Grasping the wire just above the bead, about halfway along the round-nose pliers' barrel, bend to a 90-degree angle. Move your pliers to grasp the bent tail and, with a pair of chain-nose pliers, grab the end and roll it around the barrel of the round-nose pliers to form a loop. Continue wrapping around the stem for three turns, then trim any excess and squeeze the cut end flush with chain-nose pliers.

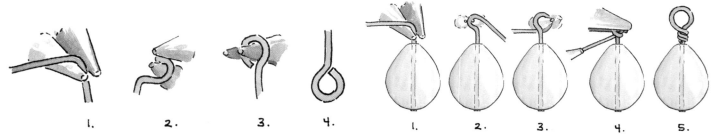

KNOTS

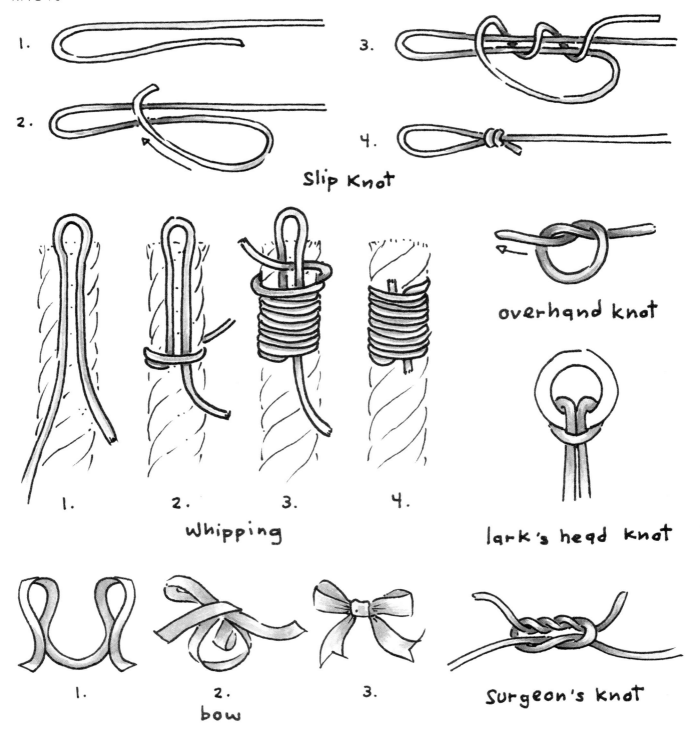

1.

2.

3.

4.

Slip Knot

1. 2. 3. 4.

Whipping

overhand knot

lark's head knot

1. 2. 3.

bow

Surgeon's knot

TEMPLATES

naiad

hammered link

hook + eye

leather feather

ivory

marbled

patina petal

resources

CRAFT

A.C. Moore—acmoore.com

Create for Less—createforless.com

Hobby Lobby—hobbylobby.com

Jo-Ann—joann.com

Michaels—michaels.com

RIBBONS, CORD + TRIM

M&J Trimming—mjtrim.com

May Arts Ribbon—mayarts.com

Tangles 'n Knots—tanglesnknots.com

Tinsel Trading—tinseltrading.com

JEWELRY SUPPLIES

Art Beads—artbeads.com

Baubles & Beads—baublesandbeads.com

Beadaholique—beadaholique.com

Beaducation—beaducation.com

Contenti—contenti.com

Fire Mountain—firemountaingems.com

Halstead—halsteadbead.com

Jewelry Supply—jewelrysupply.com

Jewelry Tools—jewelrytools.com

National Jewelers Supplies—nationaljewelerssupplies.com

Rio Grande—riogrande.com

Shipwreck Beads—shipwreckbeads.com

Toho Shoji—tohoshoji-ny.com

PLASTICS

Friendly Plastic—amaco.com/craft-jewelry-designers/friendly-plastic-retailers

Masecraft Supply—masecraftsupply.com (alternative ivory)

Sculpey—sculpey.com

Shrinky Dinks—shrinkydinks.com

VINTAGE + ANTIQUE (AND PRETTY MUCH EVERYTHING ELSE)

eBay—ebay.com

Etsy—etsy.com

Ruby Lane—rubylane.com

ART SUPPLY

Dick Blick—dickblick.com

Pearl Paint—pearlpaint.com

Utrecht—utrechtart.com

CHANDELIER CRYSTAL

Chandelier Parts—chandelierparts.com

HARDWARE

Ace Hardware—acehardware.com

Home Depot—homedepot.com

Lowe's—lowes.com

about the author

JADE GEDEON'S influences range around the world. Owing much to her family's nomadic lifestyle, she enjoyed extensive exposure to a multitude of cultures and nations growing up. Born in the United States and raised in Trinidad, she has made her home in numerous countries.

She showed a talent in drawing and fine art at a young age and went on to win a major art award. Subsequently she has displayed her work in prominent galleries, illustrated several publications and attended on scholarship one of America's most prestigious art schools, Pratt Institute. She was also invited to Denmark's Design School, where she studied in Copenhagen.

In 2002 she decided to put her artful background to work to create wonderful things. She has since sought to offer accessories that range from the quirky to the elegantly refined.

WE DREAM IN COLOUR

Handmade in the USA from materials that develop rich natural patinas, the line blends modern sensibilities with antique and vintage elements. The pieces are witty, surprising and fashioned to stand out from the crowd—ensuring the wearer sparkles from season to season. We Dream in Colour aims to create inspiring jewelry in a socially conscious fashion with minimal environmental impact.

acknowledgments

Thanks upon thanks to:

My amazing plus tax We Dream in Colour ladies who help fuel my never-ending projects.

Mika Gedeon, for being my work sidekick, sister, amazing aunty and ear to all madness.

Kathryn Gesner and Corynn Larkin—for lending their talented eyes and nimble fingers to "hold this," make, test and repeat.

My editor Marissa Giambelluca for her patience, which apparently has no end.

Designer Meg Baskis for making all those bloody pictures and words come together beautifully on paper.

Everyone at Page Street for their help and making the process so clear and surprisingly enjoyable.

My friends who let me commandeer their wrists, homes and even amazing animals (hi Maja!) for photographs.

Mom, for letting me dream.

Rhys, because, dude, you are kind of the best thing I've ever made.

index